RANDOM HOUSE

By the Fireside
CROSSWORDS

EDITED BY
STANLEY NEWMAN

**Random House
Puzzles & Games**

ISBN: 0-8129-3419-9

Random House Puzzles & Games Website address:
www.puzzlesatrandom.com

Page design and typography by Mark Frnka
Manufactured in the United States of America
2 4 6 8 9 7 5 3

First Edition

SPECIAL SALES

Random House Puzzles & Games books are available at special discounts
for bulk purchases for sales promotions or premiums. Special editions,
including personalized covers, excerpts of existing books, and corporate
imprints, can be created in large quantities for special needs.
For more information, contact Random House Special Markets at 800-800-3246.

---

1 SPENDABLES

Shirley Soloway

ACROSS

1 Sunday service
5 Curvy letter
8 Home sites
12 Prom, e.g.
13 Mormon center
15 Concerning
16 Above, with "of"
17 __ Alto, CA
18 British gun
19 Be creative, wordwise
22 Possesses
23 Singer Laine
24 Use up
26 Nutmeg kin
29 Up in __ (irate)
31 __ a Camera
32 Gabor et al.
33 Spy's org.
34 Ice-cream servers
37 Denials
38 Alters
40 Teachers' grp.
41 Impious
43 Mrs., in Madrid
44 Rind
45 Actor Wallach
46 Saloon selection
47 Sandberg of baseball
48 __ Each Other (Lombard/ Stewart film)
51 Land measure
53 Actress MacGraw
54 Pay (for)
59 Enjoy a meal
61 Ballet bend

62 Pianist Count __
63 In a while
64 Transgressions
65 Making do, with "out"
66 Repair
67 After taxes
68 In the event that

DOWN

1 __ War (racehorse)
2 Against
3 Candle brackets
4 Plant leaf
5 Feeling of elation
6 Leading player
7 Meal starters
8 Fleur-de-__
9 Exactly right
10 Delicacy
11 Logic
12 "What's up, __?"
14 Watering tool
20 Jim-dandy
21 Grand films
25 Asian language
26 Bill of fare
27 River of England
28 Took advantage of
30 Clerical residence
34 Hunt (for)
35 Hammer part
36 Shopper's draw
38 Mountain edge
39 Best of the best
42 Bullring cheer
44 Cook beforehand
46 James of Hotel
48 Call Me __
49 Skirt design
50 "Sorry about that!"
52 Dissident
55 Fork point
56 Egyptian goddess
57 Fuzz
58 Chicken part
60 Finale

2 SPREAD THE WORD

Bob Lubbers

ACROSS

1 Newspaper page
5 Nasser of Egypt
10 Story line
14 Evaluate
15 Florida city
16 Ready to pick
17 Gridlock result
19 Director Kazan
20 Prominent
21 Expert: Ger.
23 Fall behind
24 Blood line
25 Less cooked
28 Nav. rank
29 Shoelace end
33 Blackbird
34 Omelet need
35 Arm cover
36 Jazz piano pioneer
40 Inca, e.g.
41 __ Marie Saint
42 Hawaiian instrument, for short
43 Nerves of __
44 Word form for "three"
45 Something of value
47 Pro and con
49 Dallas sch.
50 One past his prime
53 Fork or spoon
57 "__, Brute?"
58 Flatter
60 Sky sight
61 The Little Mermaid
62 Hammer end
63 Crooned
64 Pee Wee or Della
65 18-wheeler

DOWN

1 Table scraps
2 Prefix for psychology
3 List ender: Abbr.
4 Pollute
5 In operation
6 Part of CPA
7 Mil. rank
8 Los __, NM
9 Less valid, as an excuse
10 Seer
11 Light rhythm
12 Mayberry boy
13 Rip
18 Dread
22 Writer Calvino
24 Fishermen
25 Mates of ranis
26 Concerning
27 Author Oscar
28 Psyche part
30 "__ pray"
31 Bring forth
32 Belief
34 Seabird
35 Wee, in Glasgow
37 Virginia town
38 Eli
39 XIV x IV
44 Term of office
45 Part of USA
46 Daybreaks
48 Prohibit
49 Stone marker
50 Dame Myra
51 "__ girl!"
52 Musial or Getz
53 Western Indians
54 Graf __
55 List entry
56 Actress Anderson
59 Make knots

3 KING'S ENGLISH

Bob Lubbers

ACROSS

1 Weaken
4 North star
11 Man in blue
14 I love: Lat.
15 Metrical foot
16 Boxing legend
17 First balcony at the Palladium
19 __-Mex cuisine
20 Journalist Bly
21 Guppy cousin
23 Most Egyptians
24 Selves
26 Oil cartel
29 Withered
30 Ski lift
31 Redden
32 Member of 26 Across
33 Threat ender
34 Adhesive tape at Chelsea Royal Hospital
39 Lake boats
40 Kelly or Disney
41 Choir members
42 Yucatán native
43 Averages
47 Assemble
48 Inlets
49 Sire
50 Staggers
52 Actor Lorne
53 Actress Ullmann
55 Washcloth at Claridge's

58 In the manner of
59 Fragrant
60 4 P.M. drink
61 Hair goo
62 Binds again
63 Wind dir.

DOWN

1 Steam baths
2 Current unit
3 Wispy tree
4 Helen's captor
5 A single time
6 Chou En-__
7 Spring mo.
8 Parish leader
9 Capri and Man
10 Manuscript marking
11 Slingshot at Harrod's

12 "Bravo!" in Barcelona
13 Snapshots, for short
18 Hamburg's river
22 Functions
24 Statesman Abba
25 Aisle at Drury Lane
27 Being: Lat.
28 *Moonstruck* star
30 Speaker of baseball
31 Pesky child
32 Turner and Pappas
33 Pueblo pot
34 Con game
35 Story

36 Intermission at Royal Albert Hall
37 Actor Robert
38 Picks up the check
42 Navy goat, e.g.
43 Hammer part
44 Ten-percenters
45 Actress Adorée et al.
46 Carved pillars
48 Grass unit
49 Copper alloy
51 Get an __ effort
52 Stickum
53 Fall behind
54 __ de France
56 Time period
57 Dandy

4 PAVING THE WAY

Fred Piscop

ACROSS

1 "Bye!"
5 College mil. group
9 Tourney type
14 Opera solo
15 Cajun-cooking vegetable
16 Baseball great Combs
17 Columnist Charen
18 Lewis novel
20 Unappetizing food
21 Phosphate mineral
22 Spider or mite
25 Central ideas
28 Refusals
29 "__ it Romantic?"
31 Brit. reference work
33 Like tartan
35 Stanford rival
36 __-bodied seaman
37 Malady
39 Southern state
41 Composer Porter
42 Two-syllable foot
44 __ point (hub)
45 Indeed
46 Dope
47 __ Antony
48 *As I Lay __* (Faulkner book)
50 Nuance
54 Guilty one
56 Swell, slangily
57 Nostalgic path
60 Bjorn of tennis
61 Without help
62 Golden-__ (senior)
63 The Preakness, for one
64 Paint type
65 T-man Eliot
66 Pervasive quality

DOWN

1 Florida city
2 Tumultuously
3 Music-publishing district
4 Battery type
5 One of Paul's Epistles
6 Giraffe relative
7 Like some chords
8 Is unable to
9 Hoopster Bob
10 __ up (rises on hind legs)
11 Blast-furnace input
12 Pub quaff
13 Encountered
19 Prepare to turn
23 Fictional ship
24 Half a dual personality
26 Caldwell classic
27 39 Across city
30 Thick slice
32 Hand out the cards
33 Type size
34 Comic actor Harold
35 Mil. branch
36 Scrub, to NASA
38 One at a time
40 Way off
43 Dock charge
46 Accustoms
47 Olympic distance measures
49 Symbols
51 Creeping plants
52 Word form for "sleep"
53 Suburbanite's gadget
55 Strategy
57 Publication, for short
58 Right-angled pipe
59 Holstein comment
60 Buddy

5 ON THE TABLE

Elizabeth Gorski

ACROSS

1 Opera solo
5 Light wood
10 Kooky
14 California city
15 E.T., e.g.
16 Double reed
17 South African
18 Glossy
19 High-schooler
20 Snappy dressers
23 Small horse
24 Center starter
25 Mount an attack
28 Down in the dumps
31 Back-to-health program, for short
35 Mrs. Kramden et al.
37 Time period
39 ". . . man __ mouse?"
40 TV reception enhancers
44 Greek vowel
45 Hither and __
46 Shrewd
47 Feel
50 Singer Cole
52 Shot for, with "at"
53 In the style of
55 Equal: Fr.
57 UFOs
63 Middling grades
64 Duck relative
65 "Bye!"
67 Actor Sean
68 Misplaces
69 All even

70 Concerning
71 Scents
72 Aware of

DOWN

1 Priest's vestment
2 Housetop
3 Concept
4 Atmospheric region
5 Washbowl
6 Bronze and pewter
7 Creditor's claim
8 Drain (into)
9 __-deep (shallow)
10 Country singer West

11 Busy as __
12 Rivals
13 Hamilton's bill
21 Vacation location
22 Spr. month
25 Manuscript enclosures: Abbr.
26 Make happy
27 Giant
29 Met Life competitor
30 Rap star Dr. __
32 Boring
33 Mountain ridge
34 Situated
36 Devious
38 Oklahoma city

41 Charged particle
42 Violinist Stern
43 Short dagger
48 Declines a proposal
49 Inventor Whitney
51 Come-on
54 __-Saxon
56 Estimate
57 Professional charges
58 Fasting period
59 Not bad
60 Not bad
61 Precipitation
62 Editor's note
63 Tax preparer: Abbr.
66 Fuss

6 ALSO-RANS

Fred Piscop

ACROSS

1 Hindu misters
5 Roy's wife
9 Nez __ Indians
14 Camping need
15 Mephistophelean
16 Rap-sheet datum
17 Goya subject
18 Synagogue scroll
19 Bird homes
20 Also-ran of '68
23 More alluring
24 World Series mo.
25 Also-ran in '28 thru '48
32 Trendy
35 Nikon rival
36 Delete
37 "Pardon me!"
39 Film genre
41 Large quantity
42 Certain flowering plant
44 Discharge
46 Writer Fleming
47 Also-ran of '80
50 Bard's "before"
51 Saudi __
55 Also-ran in '48
59 Smart folks
61 Thermometer type
62 City southeast of New Delhi
63 Staring
64 Pub serving
65 Abound
66 Cantered
67 Batter ingredient
68 London park

DOWN

1 Male deer
2 CSA general
3 Desk feature
4 Have the lead role of
5 Dissuaded
6 State positively
7 Turkish dough
8 Carrier to Tel Aviv
9 Verve
10 Certain college members
11 Get up
12 Jazz player
13 Feminine suffix
21 Earth sci.
22 Fortune
26 Stuck in the mud
27 "Nor iron bars __"
28 Finger-pointer
29 Guinea neighbor
30 On the briny
31 __ up (monopolized)
32 Trip to Mecca
33 B&O part
34 Word in many college names
38 Establish as legal tender
40 Attacks
43 Loitered
45 Pressure unit
48 New: Pref.
49 Super Bowl III hero
52 Bad news for Nicklaus
53 *The Woman* __ ('84 film)
54 "There Is Nothin' Like __"
55 Cereal noise
56 Sulk
57 Math subject
58 Put up, as a portrait
59 4 qts.
60 Self

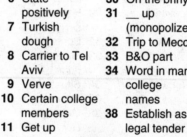

7 UNDER CONTRACT

Norma Steinberg

ACROSS

1 Sailor's call
5 Exchange
9 Cook in the microwave
12 Relocate
13 Female horses
15 Colorless
16 Publicity person
18 Small land mass
19 __ Francisco
20 Chief Exec.
21 Once-a-year
23 Cliques
24 Gator's cousin
25 Flounce about
28 Aggressive experts
32 Pencil pusher
33 Knucklehead
34 Front of the boat
35 Sitarist Shankar
36 Loose-leaf filler
37 She: Fr.
38 Revival meeting cry
39 Roman poet
40 Troll
41 Meat-case item
43 Easter hat
44 Dictionary entry
45 Strong-smelling
46 Hamilton or McGovern
49 Pierre's pop
50 Poem
53 __ mater
54 Accordion
57 Cry
58 Pachyderm teeth

59 "__ lay me down to sleep . . ."
60 Barbie's boyfriend
61 Aide: Abbr.
62 Surface depression

DOWN

1 Rock band equipment
2 Israeli dance
3 Pizzeria appliance
4 "You bet!"
5 __ pants (wise guy)
6 Salary
7 Mars' Greek counterpart
8 Pigsty

9 Actress Pitts
10 __ breve
11 Pare
14 Ignition switch
15 Miser
17 Orate
22 Negatives
23 Supermarket packaging
24 Managed, somehow
25 Tiff
26 San Antonio landmark
27 Cut
28 Music to a hitchhiker's ears
29 Synthetic fiber
30 "My mama done __ . . ."

31 Sugary
33 Solomon's father
36 Lowest-quality
40 Addams family member
42 Fireplace feature
43 Flimsiest
45 Nerds
46 Rubberneck
47 Gen. Robt. __
48 Soothsayer's clue
49 "__ in Boots"
50 Horn-section member
51 Fine feathers
52 Way out
55 Sine __ non
56 Conclude

8 SOLVE WITH E'S

Shannon Burns

ACROSS

1 German river
5 Tour again
10 *Fresh Prince of __ Air*
13 Unimportant
14 Levels out
15 French father
16 Ego
17 Looks after
18 Actress Russo
19 Become more profound
21 Less chaotic
23 Take five
24 Pince-__
25 Feel annoyed at
28 Guidelines for conduct
33 Comic DeGeneres
34 User charges
35 Flow slowly
36 Night before
37 Stimpy's pal
38 *Uno + due*
39 __ up (concludes)
41 Labor Day mo.
42 Reagan attorney general
44 Perfumes
46 __ up (admitted everything)
47 Alway
48 Not straight
49 Rode a toboggan
53 Cash in
56 Le Moko or Le Pew
57 Went hunting for morays
59 General Robert __
61 Pitcher
62 A.L. city
63 Baseball team since '62
64 B followers
65 Witch, often
66 *Peter Pan* pirate

DOWN

1 Print measures
2 Exploit
3 A Gardner
4 Grid official
5 Student's make-up
6 Occurrence
7 DC title
8 Wraps up
9 Ancient ascetics
10 Happened
11 Sea flier
12 Impolite look
15 Clinton and Coolidge, for short
20 Colonial Quaker
22 __ room
25 Singer Della
26 Santa's helpers
27 Large numbers
28 Sounds from chicks
29 Lease
30 "For __ sake!"
31 None too talkative
32 Bullock movie
34 Yours for the asking
40 Sowing machine
41 Shrill sound
42 Repair
43 Holds in high regard
45 Homer Simpson's neighbor
46 Tributary
48 Alla __
49 Plan detail
50 Indecent
51 Olympic weapon
52 Stet opposite
54 First level of sch.
55 Parcel (out)
58 Superman foe Luthor
60 Ending for legal

9 FOOD GROUPS

Randall Hartman

ACROSS

1 Musical finale
5 Understand
10 Compass point
14 Norse deity
15 German pistol
16 Ready for picking
17 "__ to Be Wild"
18 January, to Julio
19 Type of exam
20 Café freebies
23 Author Tan
24 Tool and __
25 Fragrant shrubs
29 Retain
31 NBC show since '75
34 Fighting __ (Notre Dame)
35 Author Fleming's namesakes
36 Greek portico
37 Basic foods
40 Letters on the cross
41 Swiss peaks
42 Mends, as socks
43 Your: Fr.
44 Vicinity
45 Texas city
46 Misjudge
47 Heir, often
48 Popular snack
56 Zilch
57 Seer's deck
58 Woodworker's tool
59 PDQ
60 Supply depot
61 Wife of Zeus
62 Window section
63 Like some stadiums
64 Well-groomed

DOWN

1 Actor Lee J.
2 Aroma
3 Desperate
4 __ Karenina
5 Glows
6 Like some noses
7 Matured
8 Eastern European
9 Most gratified
10 Murder, She __
11 The Emerald Isle
12 Practice boxing
13 __ Aviv
21 Russian villa
22 Gratuity
25 Boundary
26 Singer Cara
27 Prevaricators
28 Wine region
29 Fraternity letter
30 Seth's son
31 Mall unit
32 Very much
33 Cowboy's rope
35 Run in neutral
36 Night sight
38 Told the story
39 A Bell for __
44 Noah's ship
45 Pillaged
46 Run off to wed
47 Range
48 __ Verde National Park
49 Shah's domain
50 Org. formed in 1949
51 Apothecary's weight
52 Madeline of Young Frankenstein
53 Notion: Fr.
54 Poet Pound
55 Sofa or stool
56 Ray-gun blast

10 BEDDING

Lee Weaver

ACROSS

1 Seamstress Betsy
5 Summarize
10 Cotton-tipped cleaner
14 Pointed arch
15 Playing marble
16 Water main
17 Artist's tablet
19 Summer coolers
20 Auction suffix
21 Short distance
22 Run in
24 Musher's vehicle
25 Gambling machines
26 Chopped fine
29 Give way
32 Campfire remains
33 Bath adjunct
34 TV brand
35 Told a whopper
36 Gave in, in a way
37 Red and Black
38 "__ to Billie Joe"
39 Solitude seeker
40 Oil-bearing rock
41 Locations
43 Hues
44 Antiquated
45 Black-tongued dog
46 Tibetan mountain climber
48 Huron's neighbor
49 Match a raise
52 Dillon or Helm
53 Magazine's main article
56 Russian river
57 Canary sound
58 At a distance
59 Ceramic square
60 Uses a fax machine
61 Army post

DOWN

1 Took the bus
2 Folklore villain
3 Char
4 Ply a needle
5 Blew off steam
6 __ on (incited)
7 Li'l Abner's creator
8 __ premium (scarce)
9 Went by bike, in Britain
10 Athens' foe
11 Occurring over a vast area
12 Tarzan's friends
13 Most excellent
18 Capri and Man
23 Bread alternative
24 Backyard building
25 Farmer, at times
26 Circles of light
27 Out of the way
28 Tinner's supply
29 Sheltered bays
30 Map feature
31 Smooths the way
33 Piquant
36 Influential acquaintances
37 Author Irwin
39 Talk like Daffy Duck
40 Pumps, loafers, etc.
42 Hard-backed pet
43 Tees and polos
45 Doctrine
46 Plant fungus
47 Mata __
48 __-steven
49 Couch
50 Time periods
51 Rochester's wife
54 Be obligated
55 File-folder projection

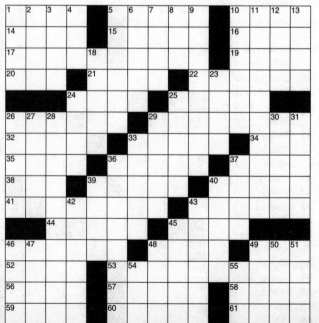

11 SAY WHAT?

Bob Lubbers

ACROSS
1 Store event
5 Unlit
9 Exchange
13 Author Hubbard
14 "Maria __" (Dorsey song)
16 Tennille or Braxton
17 Farming word form
18 Ore deposits
19 Poker payment
20 Muffet's dish
23 Lock insert
24 Chang's twin
25 Eagle nest
29 Skiing surfaces
31 Eve and Enoch
32 Thing of value
35 Like *this*: Abbr.
37 __ off (defer)
38 Warwick asked about it, in a song
42 Singer Zadora
43 Words of discovery
44 Caravan stops
45 National song
48 Quarterback Bradshaw
50 VCR button
51 *Cheers* role for Ted
52 Mil. college
55 Truck stop
60 Hip talk
63 Goose eggs
64 Swabs
65 Finished
66 January: Sp.

67 Gen. Robert __
68 Acquires
69 Group: Abbr.
70 19th-century caricaturist

DOWN
1 Not taut
2 Bicker
3 British truck
4 Oklahoma city
5 Part of FDR
6 Accompanied by
7 Comic Foxx
8 Was aware of
9 Tarried
10 Finished first
11 Picnic pest
12 Dessert choice
15 Hardwood

21 Actress Berger
22 Bowl handle
26 Some taken-back goods
27 Occupied
28 Senator Kefauver
29 Do a tailoring job
30 Ermine in summer
31 __ carte
32 One way to buy bonds
33 Polish
34 Does an usher's job
36 Evaluators
39 November veggie

40 __ *Rae*
41 Leno of late-night
46 Choppers
47 Summer: Fr.
49 Sells out, blamewise
52 String-quartet member
53 Broods
54 Map closeup
56 Verb-forming suffix
57 Actress Rowlands
58 Congressional bill: Abbr.
59 Govt. agents
60 Morning run
61 Common contraction
62 Dog's doc

PEOPLE'S CHOICE

Gerald Ferguson

ACROSS

1 Ancient Briton
5 Be a bigmouth
9 Great Pyramid, essentially
13 Resound
14 Marquis' inferior
15 Musical work
17 Chime
18 Part of A.D.
19 Complete
20 Some ring wins
23 Notes after dos
24 __-mo replay
25 Change the itinerary
29 __ in the Grass
34 Running wild
35 Spelling or Amos
36 Slugger's stat
37 Viewpoint
41 Word form for "ear"
42 Lord of the Rings creatures
43 Hill openings
44 Jolson tune
47 Brie, e.g.
48 __ de cologne
49 Rock band's initials
50 Nixonian constituency
58 In the sun, poetically
59 Long time
60 We: Fr.
62 Camp craft
63 Brownish purple
64 Fizzy drink
65 Shred
66 Hardens
67 Emcee Trebek

DOWN

1 Vigor
2 Finishes a cake
3 Bloke
4 Bridge fee
5 Defeated
6 Reels in
7 British composer
8 Political group
9 Muss, as hair
10 Choice
11 "Take __ your leader"
12 English gun
16 Letters after cues
21 Beyond peeved
22 New York town
25 Former Philippines president
26 Poet's Muse
27 Mountain climber's spike
28 Realty unit
29 Easy touch
30 Paid players
31 Go for a spin
32 Clarinets' kin
33 Washer cycle
35 __ avail (fruitless)
38 Contradict
39 Olympian blood
40 Scot's refusal
45 Actor Liam
46 Gave a tug
47 Shuts
49 Discharge
50 USAF unit
51 Construction beam
52 Country byway
53 Atlas contents
54 Fever and chills
55 Peru native
56 Implement
57 Christmas
61 Jazz instrument

13 ESSENCE OF CHANGE

Lee Weaver

ACROSS

1 Hot drink
4 Circus name
10 Feudal servant
14 Med. facilities
15 Provoke
16 "I cannot tell __"
17 Tuck's partner
18 Thin layer of metal
20 High card
21 Prescription amounts
22 Byways
23 Maui porches
25 Apple-pie baker
26 Halt at an exact point
32 Intentions
35 Storytellers
36 Rowboat need
38 Architect Christopher
39 Daffodils' origins
40 Come out second best
41 Ms. Fabray, to friends
42 Carved pin
43 Golden Rule word
44 Gridder who calls the signals
48 "I __ Rhythm"
49 Lyrical
53 E.T., e.g.
56 Part of Iberia
59 Harem room
60 Casual shoe style of the '50s
62 La Brea __ pits
63 Writer Bagnold
64 Llama with valuable wool
65 Cry of discovery
66 Computer input
67 Flew like an eagle
68 Sodom survivor

DOWN

1 Having a key, in music
2 Susan Lucci character
3 Ski resort
4 Robin Hood, for one
5 Opera passage
6 Legendary birds
7 Cook in a microwave
8 Functions
9 Tormé or Tillis
10 Lunchmeat
11 Pizazz
12 Sacred ceremony
13 Lawyer's charges
19 Trudges along
24 Trade group: Abbr.
25 War god
27 Knight's helmet decoration
28 Edmonton hockey player
29 Big shot
30 Landing spot for Neil Armstrong
31 Bridge position
32 Barley beard
33 Mideast land
34 Waiter's offering
37 Antique auto
39 Sheet of cotton
40 *Cool Hand __*
42 Sidekick
45 Planned schedule
46 Each
47 *Lord Jim* author
50 Sum
51 Sun Valley locale
52 Diamond weight
53 Mimicked
54 Melodious Horne
55 "What's __ for me?"
56 Perform without backup
57 Sobriquet for Hemingway
58 A long way off
61 __ Cruces, NM

14 SOLE SEARCHING

Bob Lubbers

ACROSS

1 Donkey
4 One way to cook beef
9 Skirt features
14 NCAA rival
15 Diplomat
16 Siouan speakers
17 Lyricist Gershwin
18 Going on a date
20 Belief
22 Word form for "blood"
23 Robot relative
26 Run-down place
31 Raid
33 Acting company
34 __ of the Sheik
36 Sign up
38 Sandy's owner
39 Sale stickers
41 French legislature
43 Crisp cookie
44 Type of poplar
46 Chopper blade
48 Electees
49 Customized
51 Generated anew
53 Fancy digs
55 Bridge blunders
58 The Supremes, e.g.
60 Nile dam
61 Showing pride
67 Skater Midori
68 A Chipmunk
69 Wished (for)
70 Ayres or Wallace
71 David's weapon
72 Adolescents
73 Arid

DOWN

1 Singer O'Day
2 Alarm
3 Taking no cards
4 Make like new
5 Canadian prov.
6 St. crosser
7 Frosh, next year
8 Word processor
9 "Ol' Blue Eyes"
10 Sea diary
11 __ Jima
12 Greek cross
13 Supersonic flyer: Abbr.
19 "__ my wits' end!"
21 Fish-eating flier
24 Charged particles
25 Challenger
27 Lots
28 Out of control
29 Bee-related
30 Chick talk
32 Giver
34 Phase
35 Desert stops
37 Slangy farewell
40 Blood fluids
42 "__, or not . . ."
45 Mosquito guard
47 Reagan and Coleman
50 Bruce or Laura
52 Scale notes
54 Vision
56 Chowhound
57 Winter forecast word
59 Western Indian
61 Is no longer
62 100%
63 XIV x IV
64 Relatives
65 Copy
66 Author Deighton

15 GO FIGURE

Eileen Lexau

ACROSS

1 300, to Caesar
4 Cabinet dept.
7 Noodles
12 Tiresome
13 Overfill
14 Peaks
15 German article
16 Verve
17 "__ all, folks!"
18 Honest one
21 Disapproving sounds
22 Your, Biblically
23 Tic-__-toe
26 Meet the bet
27 Irritates
30 Idée __
31 Cub Scout leader
32 __ and dined
33 Area of eerie disappearances
38 Cookie treats
39 Camels' features
40 Honky-__ piano
41 Shrimp dish
43 *Red October* is one
46 Boo or yoo follower
47 Big __, CA
48 Bring into harmony
50 Unpleasant repetition
54 Northern constellation
56 Coagulate
57 Bakery worker
58 Helicopter part
59 *Les États-__*
60 Prying
61 Tableau
62 Gal of song
63 Tax agcy.

DOWN

1 Coterie
2 Danish king
3 Don't play fair
4 Painter Frans
5 Western state
6 Indicate
7 Hamburger unit
8 Sore spot
9 Feeling sore
10 Asian holiday
11 Beast of burden
12 Defeats
13 Boiled
19 Uproar
20 Words of surprise
24 Skater's jump
25 Hand over
28 Neighbor of Fla.
29 Pianist Earl __ Hines
30 Shark features
31 Out of control
32 Elk
33 The two of them
34 Switch ending
35 Overhaul
36 Jamaican beverage
37 Effects
41 __ generis
42 Spring bloomer
43 Aid
44 Weasel word
45 Noah or Wallace
47 Arena posting
49 Singer Lopez
51 Computer symbol
52 Arm bone
53 Farm cover
54 AMA members
55 Mythical bird

16 SHOP TALK

Bob Lubbers

ACROSS

1 Links org.
5 Faucets
9 News summary
14 Armstrong or Simon
15 Vicinity
16 Chou __
17 Office worker
19 Begin
20 Last
21 Errs with a stopwatch
23 Predetermines
25 IBM, e.g.
26 __-bitty
27 Texas border town
29 __ Romeo (auto)
32 Hebrew, e.g.
34 Gold: Sp.
36 Blood vessels
38 __ Vegas, NV
39 Wood cutter
41 Lobe site
42 Spoils
45 Stuck-up one
46 Cause to recall
48 Greek vowels
50 Section of an org.
51 *Guys & Dolls* character
55 Dons, as a holster
58 Praised
59 Warble
60 Craft for Lindbergh
62 Contradict
63 Actress Foch
64 Not now
65 Edited out
66 Tyrolean river
67 Weeps

DOWN

1 Hungry
2 River of Paris
3 Overlays gold
4 Attu resident
5 Innate gifts
6 Exist
7 Salon jobs
8 H.H. Munro
9 Makes as good as new
10 Complete
11 Get tough
12 Swiss river
13 Peach seeds
18 Reviewer: Abbr.
22 "Beat it!"
24 Cornea cover
27 Enumerated
28 Sandwich cookie
29 Blvd. relative
30 Sitcom producer Norman
31 Emergency practice
33 Anthropologist's study
35 Sphere
37 Flecked
40 Attacks
43 Tiny soldiers
44 Astral
47 South African corn
49 "Take __!" (coach's order)
51 Author Nin
52 Moscow's state
53 Star in Cygnus
54 Barbara and Anthony
55 Ship's right side: Abbr.
56 ". . . a poem lovely as a __"
57 Atlanta stadium
61 "__ pig's eye!"

17 BAGGAGE RACK

Bob Lubbers

ACROSS

1 To the left, at sea
6 Lasting impression
10 Spanish house
14 Finger-pointer
15 Buckeye State
16 Pitcher Hershiser
17 Rifle tubes
19 Mill product
20 Yale student
21 __ *Make a Deal*
22 Earns after taxes
24 Girls
26 Reconnoiter
28 Uriah of fiction
30 Erases
34 Tra-__
37 Pilfer
39 Islands off Sicily
40 Ammonia derivative
42 Conducted
43 Attempted
44 Genesis land
45 Oklahoma city
47 Lodgings
48 Garden tools
50 Fill-in worker
52 Rhythms
54 Igneous rock
58 Generated again
61 Settled (up)
63 Actor Stephen
64 MC Trebek
65 Judicial work

68 Marathon segment
69 Raison d'__
70 Scrub a mission
71 Favorites
72 Betsy or Diana
73 Border flower

DOWN

1 Heavenly being
2 Comic Poundstone
3 Onetime Chrysler cars
4 CSA soldier
5 "Rose of __"
6 Categorize

7 Kasparov's game
8 Feel poorly
9 Gangster's gat
10 Deal (with)
11 Neighborhood
12 Char
13 __ *Well That Ends Well*
18 Alarm button
23 Director Sidney
25 Practices jabs
27 Acknowledgment
29 Most wan
31 Swellheaded
32 Garden spot
33 Caesar's namesakes

34 Final
35 Love god
36 Italian resort
38 Actor Olin
41 Arab chieftain
46 Red-ink entry
49 Bengal soldier
51 Zany
53 Prods
55 Criminal fire
56 Impolite glances
57 Succulent
58 Exitway
59 Author Wiesel
60 Sash
62 War god
66 Western Indian
67 Lawyers' org.

18 WHO'S ON FIRST

Randolph Ross

ACROSS

1 Hardwood tree
4 Shiny minerals
9 Would-be atty.'s exam
13 Way in
15 Bakery attraction
16 Author Wiesel
17 Lotion additive
18 1994 basketball documentary
20 Goes over old notes
22 Wrench target
23 Capri and Wight
24 Stylus users
25 Roll relatives
27 Director Edwards
28 Tibetan capital
29 Beantown athlete
30 Queens field
34 Part of the DOD
35 David Letterman, e.g.
38 Crew-team member
39 Campaign '96 name
41 NBA team
42 "__ a Parade"
44 Minds
46 Barrel parts
47 Dates
50 "The final frontier"
51 Seat of power
52 Landing site
55 Sing-along
57 Rock star, to a teen
58 __ of Cleves
59 Slight amount
60 Sugar source
61 __-do-well
62 Misanthrope
63 Steamed

DOWN

1 Hebrew month
2 Lone
3 Ruffians
4 Skiing brothers
5 Actor Jeremy
6 Pigeon sounds
7 Current unit
8 Miserable condition
9 Parasites
10 Quench
11 Marksman, at times
12 Trials
14 Pieces maker
19 *Billboard* category
21 Mecca Almighty
24 Immigrant's island
25 Fog up
26 Charlie Chan exclamation
27 Defeats
29 Some dorm occupants
31 Lake Mead adjunct
32 Icicle holder
33 Mars counterpart
36 Tithing amount
37 Moreno and Rudner
40 Playing marble
43 Acid in milk
45 Fish-eating flier
46 More like Mary Lou Retton
47 Allen of Vermont
48 Performed brilliantly
49 Witchlike one
50 From a previous time
52 Gray's subj.
53 NY college
54 Entreated
56 Sky altar

19

THE CAPITAL GANG

D.J. DeChristopher

ACROSS

1 Singer Lane
5 Ukrainian city
11 Iota
14 Bench, e.g.
15 Actress Meriwether
16 Bullring cheer
17 *Charlie's Angels* actress
19 Curse
20 King's chair
21 Garden activity
23 Low point
25 Friend, out west
26 One of Lear's daughters
29 Asian holiday
31 Impolite look
33 Region of Italy
35 Low digit
37 Ignore
39 Dave's TV rival
40 May birthstone
43 By way of
44 Pinnacle
46 Eggs: Lat.
47 Casino naturals
49 Pack (down)
51 Tax pro: Abbr.
53 Twilled fabric
54 Twosome
56 Fairylike
58 Greets the villain
60 More greasy
63 U.S. soldiers, for short
64 1981 US Open tennis champ
67 Hubbub
68 Magic charm
69 "Step __!"
70 Craving
71 3-D figures
72 Poet Ogden

DOWN

1 Inquire
2 Bushed
3 Immersion
4 Everlasting
5 Chan portrayer
6 Fraud
7 "A mouse!"
8 Waist cincher
9 Pry
10 Strengthen with heat
11 "Annie's Song" singer
12 Designer Cassini
13 John Ritter's dad
18 *Happy Days* daughter
22 Angers
24 Go back over
26 Punjabi prince
27 Solar/lunar year discrepancy
28 TV's Wild Bill Hickok
30 One __ customer
32 Wishing undone
34 I love: Lat.
36 Overhead trains
38 Foundation
41 Actress Gabor
42 Arnaz/Ball studio
45 Aussie birds
48 Deer meat
50 Ziti and vermicelli
52 Became boring
55 Word form for "skin"
57 Proclamations
58 Conceal
59 First king of Israel
61 Italian volcano
62 Reformer Jacob
63 Frolicsome
65 151, to Caesar
66 Ultimate degree

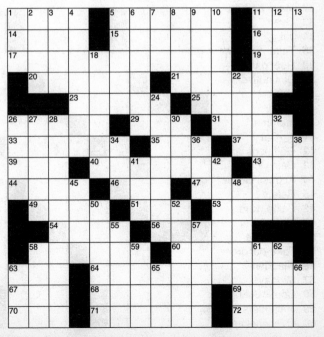

20 TAKE-OUT ORDERS

Bob Lubbers

ACROSS

1 Money
5 Goatee site
9 Brigham Young, e.g.
14 Word form for "eight"
15 Clue
16 Pacific Island group
17 Take-out order
20 __ Lingus
21 Cruising
22 Covers a wall, perhaps
23 Carney's namesakes
24 Letter opener
25 Categories
28 Twosome
29 Salamander
32 Make amends
33 Oven
34 Jai __
35 Take-out order
38 Roof part
39 Diminutive suffix
40 Water mammal
41 __-Cat
42 Golf pegs
43 Rains ice
44 Actress Goldie
45 Relate
46 Polite word
49 Maine river
50 "__ Maria"
53 Take-out order
56 Gladden
57 Midday
58 Comic Johnson
59 Jutlanders
60 Overwhelmed
61 Part of E=mc^2

DOWN

1 Caesar's partner
2 Throb
3 Mix
4 Ad __ committee
5 Bureaus
6 Gregory or Earl
7 Ancient Peruvian
8 Highest degree
9 Ascending
10 Drives down
11 Nautical direction
12 Close margin
13 Order members
18 Hoopster Abdul-Jabbar
19 Sedative
23 Golfer Palmer's nickname
24 "If You Knew __ . . ."
25 Neon and oxygen
26 Allen or Frome
27 Vibes player Red
28 Pub game
29 Type size
30 Gem surface
31 Stadium rows
33 Frequently
34 Russian cooperative
36 Shortstop Reese
37 Glob
42 Samples
43 Dueler's aide
44 It makes waste
45 Western resort lake
46 Begged
47 Pop singer Falana
48 Statesman Abba
49 Barge
50 Glow
51 American Legion members
52 Looks at
54 Genetic material
55 American uncle

21

HI AGAIN

S.N.

ACROSS

1 Theme of this puzzle
5 Nick at Nite offering
10 Leaves town
14 Type like *this*: Abbr.
15 Last Greek letter
16 Springy tune
17 A good way to take bad news
20 Sunday speech: Abbr.
21 What the particular may pick
22 British cattle breed
23 "Zip-__-Doo-Dah"
24 Iowa city
25 Sun worshiper
28 Iowa city
29 Actor Holbrook
32 Vision-related
33 Struck down, old-style
34 A few
35 Treats casually
38 Moves quickly
39 Suspicious
40 Tilted
41 Commercials, for instance
42 Cindy Crawford ex
43 Colloquial
44 Hostile criticism
45 Tim of *WKRP*
46 *It All Started with Columbus* author
49 *Misery* star
50 Recipe phrase
53 Tropical Asian shrub
56 Take care of
57 Occupied
58 Shatner's best-known role
59 Nintendo rival
60 "A Boy __ Sue"
61 Midmonth day

DOWN

1 Haunches
2 __ *Jury* (Spillane novel)
3 It may be over your head
4 Under the weather
5 More optimistic
6 Overact
7 Sales personnel
8 "That's gross!"
9 Basketball inventor
10 Windshield material
11 Portrait medium
12 High-fashion mag
13 Underworld river
18 Next to bat
19 Stage signals
23 Sheriff Lobo portrayer
24 *Jaws* town
25 Former South African prime minister
26 Plant pest
27 Pigs' digs
28 Love, Italian-style
29 *"Crocodile" Dundee* star
30 In the midst of
31 Southpaw
33 Lewis Carroll beast
34 Golf Hall-of-Famer
36 Does an inaugural job
37 Champaign athletes
42 Substance on stamps
43 Ocean floor
44 Mrs. Ted Turner
45 Uplift
46 New Testament book
47 '50s president of South Korea
48 Flash Gordon foe
49 Buddy
50 Corrosive chemical
51 Entice
52 Pops the question
54 Aunt in *Bambi*
55 Travel downhill, in a way

22 SWEET TALK

S.E. Wilkinson

ACROSS

1. Like Kojak
5. Prefix for "chute"
9. MacLeod of *Love Boat*
14. Get an __ effort
15. General Bradley
16. In reserve
17. A-one auto
19. Club rule
20. "__ I Know" (Whitney Houston tune)
21. Photographer Ansel
22. Gut busters
25. Legendary engineer Jones
26. Deferred promise
30. Fly high
31. Orient
32. Grade-school grp.
35. Noted middleweight
40. Sellout sign
41. CBer's radio
42. Propagated
43. Lead-pipe cinch
47. Former foe of Ilie and Jimmy
50. Opening remark
51. Sensational
52. Castle feature
57. Match up
58. *Planes, Trains and Automobiles* star
60. From then on
61. Criticism
62. Folksinger Burl
63. All fired up
64. "K-K-K-__"
65. Harp kin

DOWN

1. Big name in baroque music
2. Bushy do
3. Theater magnate Marcus
4. Make a sketch
5. Sturdy fabric
6. Magic charm
7. Brit. fliers
8. Comment from Sandy
9. Revisit
10. Imminently
11. Tennis pro Guillermo
12. Start of Caesar's boat
13. Fit to print
18. Skirt length
23. Apt anagram for THE EYES
24. Close up
26. Decant
27. Shakespearean villain
28. Historic period
29. It's polar to NNW
30. Draft agcy.
32. Boston Common, e.g.
33. Lumber source
34. Figure up
36. Dancer's gang
37. *Norma* __
38. Parisian landmark
39. Celtics' org.
43. The artist formerly known as The Artist
44. Outdated
45. Gofer
46. Dense mixture: Abbr.
47. Apathetic
48. __ Ward Howe
49. Gasket
53. '50s sitcom star Storm
54. Green-eyed monster
55. Frankfurt's river
56. It's at 11 Wall St.
58. Controversial Oliver Stone film
59. Suffix for scram

23 ANATOMICALLY CORRECT

Bill Hendricks

ACROSS

1 Bit of gossip
5 Garb for Snoopy, sometimes
10 Resembling, with "to"
14 Word form for "far"
15 Moon-related
16 Attend a banquet
17 Flee
20 Mel of diamond fame
21 Acting part
22 Salespersons' goals
23 Gladys Knight's backup
25 Burger breads
26 Begley Sr. and Jr.
27 Hard journey
28 Beret, for instance
31 Lost
34 Any time now
35 As seen fit
36 Get ready to order a martini
39 Vientiane's land
40 Noisy
41 Too big
42 Part of i.e.
43 Streetcorner sign
44 Miss Piggy, self-referentially
45 "No pain, no __"
46 Unable to leave
50 Start of a Stephen Foster title
53 Treacherous
54 Meadow
55 Tackles et al.
58 Cartwright son
59 Rib
60 Rim
61 Muscle quality
62 Sign up for
63 Gardener's purchase

DOWN

1 *Some Like __*
2 Saw parts
3 Gladden
4 Garment-tag abbr.
5 Fore-and-aft riggers
6 Shirley Temple trademark
7 Feed the kitty
8 Cheerleader's cry
9 Habituate
10 Pedro's parting word
11 It's worn with a sporran
12 *To Live and Die __*
13 TV T-man
18 Literary manservant
19 Male model, maybe
24 Banana eaters' garbage
25 Big family
27 Find the sum
28 One of a pair of dice
29 "Oh, woe!"
30 Combustible heap
31 Competent
32 Sri Lankan exports
33 Vegas machine, for short
34 Cereal utensil
35 Left-side entry
37 Final
38 Big to-do
43 Swedish car
44 "The Manassa __" (Jack Dempsey)
45 "Understand?"
46 Small thicket
47 __-France (former province)
48 Brink
49 Lessened
50 "__ first you don't succeed . . ."
51 Behind-the-times type
52 Colorful horse
53 Insipid
56 Actor Cariou
57 Affirmative vote

24 ALL BUSINESS

Ed Julius

ACROSS

1 Historical periods
5 Car accessory
10 Soviet news agency
14 Function
15 Parenthetical comment
16 Jai __
17 Economic forces
20 Give evidence in court
21 With 60 Down, popular pet
22 Actress Merkel
23 Suffix for comment
24 Short-term promissory note
33 One __ time (singly)
34 Sea eagles
35 French resort
36 Poet Teasdale
38 Author Philip's family
40 Sandwich shop
41 Seed covering
42 Get ready, for short
43 Was a candidate
44 Software specialists
49 Map abbreviation
50 Corp. bigwig
51 Alleviate
55 Chemical catalyst
59 EDP equipment
61 Colonizing creatures
62 Andes beast
63 Be prevalent
64 Nearly all
65 Like some cereals
66 Mah-jongg piece

DOWN

1 Prefix for while
2 Bounder
3 European range
4 Anatomical partition
5 Traveler on foot
6 Londoner's exclamation
7 Wrestler's goal
8 Teachers' degs.
9 Phone button
10 __ *the Bachelor* ('57 film)
11 Wings: Lat.
12 __ *souci* (carefree)
13 Beef quantity
18 One-dimensional figure
19 O.K. Corral battler
24 Houses, in Hermosillo
25 Eared seal
26 Homer hitter Roger
27 Farmer's concern
28 Prefix for mural
29 Pale
30 Seashore structures
31 Brilliant success
32 Bridle attachments
37 Unselfish one
39 Astronaut
45 Coup d'__
46 Prefix for maniac
47 Jump
48 Dairy product
51 Economist Smith
52 __-Japanese War
53 Bilko and York: Abbr.
54 First name in jazz
55 1960 Summer Olympics site
56 Needle case
57 Singer Carter
58 Kilmer poem subject
60 See 21 Across

25 MEN OF THE MONTH

S.N.

ACROSS

1 "I __ Little Prayer"
5 Parisian pals
9 Coffee/chocolate combo
14 Energy source
15 Earth sci.
16 Spheres of interest
17 '80s Big Apple boss
20 Saw wood, so to speak
21 Deeply held
22 Wild blue yonder
23 "__ girl!"
25 The Bee __ (rock group)
27 Giant Hall-of-Famer
31 Annapolis sch.
35 Former ring king
36 High-schooler
37 Magazine exec
39 Melodic
41 P.M. periods
43 "__ you so!"
44 Tied up
46 Agenda component
48 Sugar Loaf Mountain city
49 Split apart
50 Meat magnate
53 Nightclub in a Manilow tune
55 Rod attachment
56 May honoree
59 Spartan slave
61 Conductor Sir Georg
65 Clinic founders
68 More mad
69 Appearance
70 __ above the rest (superior)
71 Greek letter
72 Cries of fright
73 "__ a Lady" (Tom Jones tune)

DOWN

1 Antiaircraft weapons: Abbr.
2 __ end (concluded)
3 It has its ups and downs
4 Unscrupulous
5 Sweet 16, e.g.
6 Public-relations people
7 "I would give everything __ . . ."
8 Colloquial
9 *The Treasure of the Sierra* __
10 Where Mork and Mindy honeymooned
11 Corp. board members
12 Cab driver
13 Pale
18 Give a new name to
19 Singer Della
24 Golf area
26 Work wear
27 Jack and Jill's quest
28 "The Man __" (Gershwin tune)
29 Closet contents
30 Funny business
32 Tale
33 "I'm telling the truth!"
34 Intensity of emotion
38 Least distinct
40 C __ (Pepsi rival)
42 Sci-fi phenomenon
45 Bashful's brother
47 Before, in poems
51 Biblical temptress
52 Honolulu hellos
54 *Pal Joey* co-librettist
56 __ Helens, WA
57 Words of dread
58 Nothing more than
60 Off-Broadway award
62 Mr. Walesa
63 Rightful
64 Adherents: Suff.
66 Encountered
67 Light-switch positions

26 SENSE OF DIRECTION

Frances Hansen

ACROSS

1 Vein contents
5 Three-note chord
10 Vending-machine opening
14 Deep black
15 Up high
16 First name in architecture
17 Fish alternative
18 Skirt styles
19 Periodic table datum: Abbr.
20 Midmorning
22 Disregard
24 Spot for a shade
27 Chestnut shade
28 Five-star monogram
30 ". . . sickness __ health"
31 Garage job
34 Director Howard
35 Hungarian dog
36 Snappish
37 Hill builders
39 Feathered talker
42 Synagogue
43 *Throw __ From the Train*
45 Seize
47 "__ You Lonesome Tonight?"
48 Wholesale
50 Dimensions
51 Aetna's bus.
52 "I've __ Feeling I'm Falling"
53 "Old Rough and Ready"
55 Flag of France
58 *Waiting for __*
61 Ho Chi __
62 Navratilova rival
65 Dame Chaplin
66 Minimizing ending
67 Take care of
68 One in debt
69 Some votes
70 Matriculate
71 __ even keel

DOWN

1 Went out
2 Mitch Miller's instrument
3 Vaudeville song
4 Chou __
5 Beret kin
6 Slugger's stat
7 Tony Blair's home
8 Tel __
9 Sandy land
10 Liner routes
11 Speak candidly
12 *Answer Yes __* (old game show)
13 Swiped
21 Queue before Q
23 Debacle
25 Beat it
26 Smooth of speech
28 Theater fare
29 "__ go gentle . . ."
32 Roadster reversal
33 Ernie and Gomer
38 Kisses
40 Pavarotti piece
41 Blurred
44 In the matter of
46 Neth. neighbor
49 *Thy Neighbor's Wife* author
54 New-car odometer reading
55 Feds
56 Multitalented Moreno
57 Ceramist's need
59 Draftable
60 Mountain lake
63 U.S. 80, for one
64 Craggy peak

27 FLOWER POWER

Fred Piscop

ACROSS

1 Small fights
6 City of Light
11 __ Plaines, IL
14 __ once (in unison)
15 One-celled creature
16 Quantity: Abbr.
17 1964 top-10 song
19 Drink cubes
20 Stadium section
21 Confused
23 Year-end singer
27 Passed along
29 Battery terminals
30 __ Abdul-Jabbar
31 Late __ (sleepyhead)
32 1995 NFL MVP Brett
33 Mischievous one
36 AAA recommendations
37 Exposes
38 Muse of history
39 Tie up the phone
40 New __, CT
41 Asks opinions
42 Phonograph inventor
44 Tranquil
45 Animal trainer
47 Encouraged
48 Synthetic fiber
49 Carson predecessor
50 French land mass
51 "Keep it a secret!"
58 G-man
59 Mennonite
60 Until now
61 Unspecified number
62 Ill-natured
63 Lenient one

DOWN

1 Kids' game
2 "Well, __ be!"
3 Jeb Bush's state: Abbr.
4 Hula hoop, for one
5 __ Brothers (country band)
6 Less ruddy
7 Latin love
8 Minister, for short
9 "How Can __ Sure" (1967 tune)
10 Pound-cake name
11 Henry James novel
12 Show's host
13 Lieu
18 Fibber's repertoire
22 __ kwon do
23 Tote
24 Singer O'Day
25 Presidential mom
26 Shelley works
27 Poe bird
28 Drops the ball
30 Actress Black
32 Be partial to
34 Pooh's creator
35 Sat, as a model
37 Army post
38 Apple center
40 Mountain dweller
41 Noblewoman
43 Ike's monogram
44 Onetime Iranian ruler
45 Israeli port
46 "Over the Rainbow" composer Harold
47 Noseless comic-strip figure
49 "Hey, you!"
52 Actress Thurman
53 Scale notes
54 Pay court to
55 Inactive
56 Act the stoolie
57 Prohibitionist

28 MAKING CONTACT

Rich Norris

ACROSS

1. Created
5. Fine rain
9. Type styles
14. October birthstone
15. Wile E. Coyote's supplier
16. __ board (manicurist's need)
17. Reps' check-in area
19. Aphorism
20. Where negotiations stall
22. Crumpets companion
23. Bed-and-breakfast
24. Duster's need
27. Canyon effect
30. Joins, as for a meeting
35. Perry's creator
37. Mad Hatter associate
39. Fishing net
40. Parts of a farewell speech, perhaps
43. Word in Kansas' motto
44. Lady of Spain
45. Get together
46. Consequence
48. Pusher chaser
50. Kildare and Welby: Abbr.
51. "Of course!"
53. __ banana (star comic)
55. Some two-family residences
63. More devious
64. Setting the standard
65. Did a personnel job
66. Make hay?
67. Bone above the ankle
68. Stiff collars
69. Prayer ending
70. Actress Sommer

DOWN

1. Tree-trunk growth
2. Give __ on the back
3. Painter Salvador
4. Put into office
5. Mexican musician
6. Computer symbol
7. Urban health concern
8. Adagio, allegro, etc.
9. NOW's movement
10. Muscat's country
11. Cry at a bakery
12. Baseball Hall-of-Famer Speaker
13. Beethoven work: Abbr.
18. __-ball (arcade game)
21. Switch positions
24. Pave anew
25. Came up
26. Excessive supplies
28. Farm worker
29. Church instrument
31. Jazz or Heat
32. Fathered
33. Signer, slangily
34. Bird houses
36. Light brown
38. Writer Bombeck
41. Hoisting lines, in sailing
42. Extraterrestrial's term of address?
47. Private eye, briefly
49. Farm house?
52. Biblical queen's domain
54. Throb steadily
55. Came down
56. Beginner
57. High-schooler
58. Test
59. Wipe out of a manuscript
60. Humorist Mort
61. Estrada of *CHiPs*
62. "Auld Lang __"
63. That woman

29 PRIZE PACKAGE

Wayne R. Williams

ACROSS

1 Play part
4 Goes too fast
10 Criminal, to a cop
14 Virgo preceder
15 Hoi __
16 Sea green
17 __ Cruces, NM
18 Lacking recognition
19 Lays (down)
20 1992 Olympics gold-winning lightweight
23 Leavening agent
24 Fish sauce
27 Long-time FBI head
32 Group of rooms
33 Flap lips
36 Makes one
38 Any time now
39 Afore
40 Jerry Mathers' costar
42 U-turn from SSW
43 Louis and Carrie
45 Poetic comparison
46 Stitch
47 Hemp fiber for caulking
49 Military students
51 Listless
53 Monarch's loyal subject
57 *Trio* singer with Parton and Ronstadt
62 Unpaid-debt biz
64 Explanation
65 Breakfast drinks, for short
66 Team in a yoke
67 Have in mind
68 Female rabbit
69 Rocky crags
70 Lads' mates
71 After-dusk time, to a poet

DOWN

1 Combination of metals
2 Come to a halt
3 Puccini opera
4 Gush forth
5 Lake's smaller cousin
6 Otherwise
7 Hebrew month
8 Lady of Spain
9 Eyeful
10 Early paper
11 Math expressions
12 Road track
13 __ de deux
21 Cigar residue
22 W. Hemisphere grp.
25 Make amends
26 Continue a subscription
28 Yoko's family
29 Of wine
30 Former forms of words
31 Made over
33 Italian port
34 Indo-Iranian
35 Honey farmer
37 Shoe part
41 Marshy nesting areas
44 Legal order
48 Demure, in London
50 Knight's address
52 Actor Ritchard
54 Wear away
55 Military doll
56 Ruhr Valley city
58 Singer Horne
59 Cereal grains
60 Employs
61 Sharpen
62 Go bad
63 Word form for "outer"

30 DIAMOND CALLS

Rich Norris

ACROSS
1 Hawaiian singer
6 Kids' ball material
10 Does something
14 "So long, Juan!"
15 Track shape
16 Farce
17 Angry tenants' tactic
19 Curbside call
20 Bklyn. campus
21 Superman foe Luthor
22 Pitcher Hershiser
23 Most painful
27 Musical encore
29 #1 Son's dad
30 Madrid Mrs.
32 "Just __" (Nike slogan)
33 Pilaf ingredient
34 Actor LaRue
36 Satisfy completely, as a debt
39 Moose relative
40 Gentle breezes
42 Pal, slangily
43 Paris river
45 Toon skunk Le Pew
46 Tail maneuvers
47 Get close to
49 Cal. neighbor
50 Pub pints
51 Fought for a lower price
54 Brandon of *Shane*
56 __-Romeo (imported auto)
57 Brother of Dopey
59 Spill the beans
60 Support the home team
61 Annual rural event

66 Andrew of *Melrose Place*
67 Card-game fee
68 Ruckus
69 Holbrook and Linden
70 Dennis the Menace, at times
71 Swashbuckler Flynn

DOWN
1 __ es Salaam
2 Poetic tribute
3 Diarist Anaïs
4 Washington-to-Moscow connection
5 Actor Davis
6 Partner of neither
7 Partner of good

8 Suburbanite, in the fall
9 Showed one's muscles
10 Queens community
11 Certain gala dance
12 April concerns for many
13 Happy expression
18 Vigorous fight
23 Farmland units
24 Argentina neighbor
25 Basketball violation
26 Maria von __
28 Goes like the weasel?
31 Pale
35 Promoted with flair

37 More than suggested
38 Deputized group
40 Enthusiasm
41 Go back (to)
44 Denies the existence of
46 Anticipate the arrival of
48 Depot porter
51 Like Alaskan winters
52 "So long, 1 Across!"
53 *Lorna* __
55 Bruce __ (Batman)
58 Uses a scissors
62 Bottom line
63 Make public
64 Word form for "equal"
65 Family member: Abbr.

31 DO ME A FLAVOR

S.N.

ACROSS

1 Castle protector
5 Lasting impression
9 Sitcom set in Korea
13 Big name in talk TV
15 Mulligan-stew maker
16 Actress Chase
17 Center of attraction
18 Top draws in poker
19 Profit
20 Toll-house cookie ingredients
23 Krazy __
24 Exerciser's surface
25 Most resolute
29 From a great distance
31 Sound of recognition
34 Verdi specialty
35 Cloudless
36 Steel source
37 Fair-haired one
40 Sushi-bar selections
41 Physicist's tidbit
42 Fudd or Gantry
43 Prefix for long or now
44 CATs do it
45 Punishment personified
46 __ leaf cluster (medal extra)
47 Sup
48 Cake flavoring
56 Actress Moran or Gray
57 Skillful
58 Oldtime anesthetic
60 Clock sound

61 Night, in Normandy
62 Prince Harry's mama
63 Selections from Shelley
64 Party giver
65 Helen of __

DOWN

1 Mr. __ (househusband film)
2 Oil cartel
3 Get one's back up
4 Southwestern snack
5 Commandment verb
6 *Your Show of Shows* costar
7 Help a hood
8 George Clooney's aunt
9 Power
10 Jai __
11 Leap lightly
12 Holbein or Brinker
14 Metal cutter
21 Feedbag bit
22 Traffic component
25 Visit
26 Comparatively competent
27 Actress Oberon
28 Historical periods
29 Composer Copland
30 Unyielding
31 Sweet smell
32 Made sharp
33 Conductor Previn

35 Greek cheese
36 What Pandora unleashed
38 Adverse reaction
39 Color of embarrassment
44 Actor Mineo
45 "Can't Help Lovin' __ Man"
46 Sty's cries
47 Bring to bear
48 Put the kibosh on
49 Much too dry
50 Well-bred
51 Peek-__
52 Connecticut collegians
53 Working hard
54 Treat coal
55 ". . . a __'clock scholar"
59 Bit of sunshine

32 FAMILIAR QUOTATIONS

David Owens

ACROSS

1 Former Teamsters head
6 Melville South Seas novel
10 Ultra-violet-blocking chemical
14 "__ and hungry look"
15 Refuses to
16 First man
17 Towel fabric
19 Story
20 Piano piece
21 X-ray discoverer
23 Annoying noises
25 Bedtime rituals
26 "What a good boy __"
29 Doorstep drier
30 "Yes, it was spelled wrong!"
31 Backfire
35 Words to Macduff
39 Roman censor
40 Dickens title character
42 Rosebud's owner
43 Bean pole
45 Underwater swimmer
47 Allow
49 $5 bill
50 Hallucinogenic letters
51 Tom and Diane
55 Rushed
57 Grouchy?
59 Iran's former name
63 "Alice's Restaurant" name
64 Sweet snack
66 Sweet person
67 Helen of Troy's mother
68 "Walk __ in My Shoes"
69 Go after flies
70 Venerable British school
71 Tops of heads

DOWN

1 Bowlers and derbies
2 Butter alternative
3 Flowerless plant
4 Electrical unit
5 Whenever
6 Barn bird
7 Othello, for one
8 Winning
9 The "al." in et al.
10 Kids' game
11 Words of wisdom
12 Harvest machine
13 Endings to 25 Across
18 False story
22 Hammer target
24 Autograph hound's quarries
26 Basics
27 Circle of water
28 Little bit
32 Picture-hook device
33 __ compos mentis
34 Blunders
36 "__ come back now, hear?"
37 Cash-drawer compartment
38 Bookworm, maybe
41 Mawkish
44 Singer/actor Howard
46 Patella
48 Extra-base hit
51 An abundance
52 Street-sign shape
53 Half a Washington city's name
54 Shooter's sport
56 Serious show
58 Word form for "inner"
60 Agitated state
61 Doing nothing
62 Roll-call count
65 A Bobbsey

33 TIME FRAMES

R.H. Wolfe

ACROSS
1 Gives __ on the back
5 Capital of Bangladesh
10 Reach across
14 Main course
15 How tuna may be packed
16 Military force
17 Rarely
20 Bad weather
21 *Green Mansions* bird-girl
22 One way to cook
23 Pace
24 Deters
26 Cortez's quest
28 Eye makeup
32 Indian noble
37 Triumphant cries
38 Long time
42 Whistle sound
43 Relaxes from work
44 Phases
48 "Can I help you?"
49 Challengers
51 Male turkeys
55 Line of fashion?
58 Casino city
59 Make effervescent
61 Occasionally
64 Soft-drink flavoring
65 Fear
66 Give birth to
67 Trudge
68 Fergie's first name
69 Bullring cheers

DOWN
1 Hubbubs
2 Cream containers
3 British racing site
4 Yonder
5 Rackets
6 Santa __, CA
7 Dangerous snake
8 Eyelash
9 Vassar grad, perhaps
10 Americans' Uncle
11 Univ. title
12 Love: Lat.
13 Manhattan, to the P.O.
18 Article from abroad
19 Packs away
24 Karate school
25 A whole bunch
27 The old college cry
29 *The Man Who Mistook His Wife for __*
30 Comedienne Martha
31 Part of NAACP
32 __ Hari
33 Cookiemaker Wally
34 Skirt shape of yore
35 Started the kitty
36 Astern
39 "Simon __"
40 Waikiki strings
41 In hierarchical sequence
45 Mae's *She Done Him Wrong* costar
46 Economist's evaluations
47 Spanish woman
50 Crew-team member
52 Word form for "straight"
53 Taj __
54 Canyon of comics
55 Give a leg up
56 Not good
57 Note at the office
59 S __ (green-stamp issuer)
60 Chemical endings
62 Bolshevik's color
63 Highest bond rating

34 HARD PLACES

S.N.

ACROSS

1 Utters
5 Vigoda and Lincoln
9 Uninteresting
13 Skirt fold
15 Oliver Twist's request
16 Increased
17 Kuklapolitan player
18 Perry Mason portrayer
19 Feel sore
20 Environmental problem
22 Rubberneck
24 MGM's mascot
25 __ Three Lives
26 __ facto
27 Gets hitched
29 Get an __ effort
31 Half a pendulum's path
34 "__-daisy!"
36 Farm unit
38 Church instrument
40 Aquarium fish
42 Expert
43 Unknowing
44 "Moving right __ . . ."
45 Game played at and with clubs
47 Radioer on wheels
48 Coop dweller
49 December song
51 Cake finisher
53 Heaven on earth
55 Whitish gem
57 "__ was saying . . ."
60 Elfin
62 Gave a new name to
64 Tide type
65 Blind as __
67 Roadside accommodations
68 War god
69 Junction point
70 Hold responsible
71 Nevada town
72 Way out
73 __ Scott Decision

DOWN

1 Ersatz coffee table
2 Kate & __ (sitcom)
3 Old Faithful's home
4 Je ne __ quoi
5 Mosey
6 National Bureau of Standards headquarters
7 Blow it
8 Musician Mendes
9 Challenges the top gun
10 Symbol of solidity
11 Carolina county
12 It may be Lite or dark
14 Unenthusiastic
21 Ingrid's *Casablanca* role
23 Cook wear
28 Get through hard work
30 Believe
32 Four-star review
33 Singular sensation
34 A Four Corners state
35 Retired soccer star
37 Cashier's workplace
39 Dash, for example
41 Actress Moorehead
46 Italian auto
50 In stock
52 Make an ascent
54 Sot, for short
56 Flying Pan
58 "Why don't you come up and __"
59 Avoided work
60 "I didn't know I had it __"
61 Ground grain
63 Ratted (on)
66 Scare word

35 BODY DOUBLES

S.N.

ACROSS

1 What you eat
5 Evert of tennis
10 Close-fitting
14 Christie or Karenina
15 Some are dyeing to get it
16 Turnpike payment
17 Consecutive
19 In the matter of
20 Takes the wheel
21 Auto accessories
23 Internalize anger
26 Moreno and Coolidge
27 Three-seaters of a sort
30 Physique, for short
31 Card game
32 Three __ match
33 Reducing salons
35 Grandma's hat
38 Osso __ (Italian entrée)
40 Sheik's home
42 Scotch partner
43 Squanders
45 Thumbs-down answers
47 Drink a bit
48 Device named for its shape
49 Yoko __
50 Assist in crime
52 Swan relative
54 Beach bungalow
56 Who's home?
58 Logical method
62 Heavy metal
63 Kind of combat
66 Come to grips with
67 TV studio sign

68 Passion personified
69 Winter transportation
70 Pace
71 Ltr. enclosure

DOWN

1 Applies lightly
2 __ the finish (competitive to the end)
3 Ending for insist or persist
4 *The Farmer __ Wife* (Henry Fonda's first film)
5 Went for
6 Isr. lang.
7 Cell substance
8 Snuck up slowly
9 Welfare
10 Subway stops
11 Virtually even
12 Extreme
13 Photo finish
18 Lock of hair
22 Singer Guthrie
24 Way up the slopes
25 Praise, in a mass
27 Bawls
28 "Come __!" (invitation of a sort)
29 In person
34 Mas' mates
35 Tournament qualifying exemption
36 Fix sloppy copy

37 "Lights out" music
39 Partial
41 Simp
44 Range player of song
46 Sony competitor
49 Gas rating
51 Big parties
52 Comes out swinging?
53 *Love Story* star
55 Lone Star baseballer
57 Expended
59 Mitchell mansion
60 Monkey in space
61 Store gds.
64 *Platoon* setting
65 Potato-chip partner

36 RHYME TIME

Karen Hodge

ACROSS

1 Strong __ ox
5 Frank
9 Tree trunk's cover
13 New pilot's milestone
14 Playwright O'Casey
15 Calcutta cash
16 Ability-based donation
18 Plot twist, perhaps
19 Letters on an urban sign
20 Savoir faire
21 Goes along
22 Oscar de la __
24 Show-off
26 "Fine!"
28 Makes a decision
29 Trendy bunch
32 Goes wrong
33 Decrease
36 Word of regret
37 Martini's vermouth-making partner
39 Went quickly
40 Cake makings
41 D.C. daily
42 Where to get beer on board
44 Weakens
45 Monterrey money
46 Unreasonable, as prices
48 Adored ones
52 __ cat (fearful one)
54 Verdi opera
56 Deli meat
57 Kemper competitor
58 Wallflower, possibly
60 Like cacti
61 Building wings
62 Face shape
63 Ritzy
64 Ritzy
65 Mousetrap need

DOWN

1 __ as the eye can see
2 Italian wine
3 Man from Mars
4 "__ iron bars a cage"
5 Workplace watchdog grp.
6 Great
7 Keeps an __ the ground
8 Compass pt.
9 Grand Canyon transportation
10 "You're __ and don't know it"
11 Philospher Descartes
12 Props for Captain Kangaroo
15 Arrestee's demand
17 Investment
21 Attribute
23 Play horseshoes
25 Resurfaces roads
27 Progressive decline
29 Jazzmen's session
30 Whitney family patriarch
31 Returns calculation
32 Winter hours in St. Pete
33 Dopey's house-mate
34 Novelist Levin
35 For every
38 Word form for "bone"
39 Walked on
41 Check time
43 Flu variety
44 Like a beanpole
45 Little bottles
46 "__ Doll" (Ellington tune)
47 Wine giant
49 Butler's wife
50 Polynesian porch
51 Make metal
52 Eat not
53 Payment-misser's risk, for short
55 China piece
58 Get-up-and-go
59 Exemplar of patience

37 HATS ENTERTAINMENT

Ann Masten

ACROSS

1 Works hard
6 Oxford, for example
10 Cartoonist Al
14 Circa
15 From Ger.
16 Small, sweet sandwich
17 Don Carter's six-time title
20 Aquarium performer
21 Publicity piece
22 Poker payment
23 "__ fair in love and war"
24 Eastern European
27 Lose firmness
29 Whistle sound
33 Kiddie colorer
36 Bottle part
39 IV squared
40 "A drop of golden sun"
41 What's left
43 Watering hole
44 GI's hangout
45 Rock tune's attraction
46 Embryonic cell
48 Nota __
50 "I don' wanna!"
52 Was obligated to
53 Wander around
56 PDQ
59 School hymn
62 Thomas Jefferson was one
66 Smashing sport of a sort

68 Champagne bucket
69 Singer/actress Carter
70 Large family
71 What "sic" means
72 Medal metal
73 Sesame Street grouch

DOWN

1 File-folder parts
2 One of the winds
3 Corn country
4 A little night music
5 Suds mug
6 Boulders
7 Mag magnate, for short
8 Angry
9 Waters of song
10 Least direct
11 Neighborhood
12 Dinner veggies
13 Read carefully (over)
18 Deteriorate
19 House addition
24 Wash well
25 Undo
26 Polyester partner
28 Actress Ekberg
30 *The __ Incident* (Fonda film)
31 Sort of round
32 Pooped
34 Celestial sphere
35 At birth
37 Slangy relative

38 Crucial
42 California city
47 Errand boys
49 Fielder's bane
51 Prince of the theater
54 *Dynasty* commodity
55 Doing great on
57 DC VIP
58 Increase, as a collection
59 Mine passage
60 Car repairer, for short
61 Big bird
63 Norse explorer
64 Statesman Eban
65 Specialty hairdresser
67 Under the weather

38 QUESTIONNAIRE

Penny A. Roman

ACROSS

1 Roman wear
6 Mix and Selleck
10 Impresses a lot
14 Rub out
15 Smell __ (be suspicious)
16 Tea-time talk
17 Question in a kids' game
19 Carry around
20 Ending for expert
21 Guffaw, à la Variety
23 Put in stitches
24 "Ay, __ the rub"
27 Loafer, for instance
29 Least praiseworthy
30 British school of fame
31 Like sushi
32 Distributed, as cards
35 They may be convertible
38 St __'s Fire
40 Put away for later
42 Pouched bread
43 Like some turkeys
45 Hogs' homes
47 Short Line and B&O
48 Roll of stamps
50 Passes by
52 Rings up
54 Earmark
55 Paw's wife
56 Engineering school, for short
58 Deteriorate
59 Suffix for smash or stink

61 Bugs Bunny's question
66 See 40 Across
67 "Are not!" response
68 Stupendous sales
69 Alter ego of fiction
70 "__-ho and a bottle . . ."
71 Actress Berger

DOWN

1 President pro __
2 Acapulco gold
3 Gangster's gun
4 Comparatively pale
5 Is furious
6 Highlands hat
7 Evangelist Roberts
8 Mexican Amerinds
9 Restrain
10 Play part
11 Lou Costello's question
12 Gone from the plate
13 One-pot dinner
18 __ Pieces (candy)
22 Goes well with
24 ". . . and __ a good night"
25 Start of a tongue-twister question
26 Sports data
28 The lowdown
29 Get ready for a quiz
33 Auctioneer's unit

34 Gave it a whirl
36 ". . . a poem lovely as __"
37 Backtalk
39 Melville novel
41 Specialty fishermen
44 Beer order
46 Enjoys fish and chips
49 Margin for error
51 Chicken dish
52 Fun gathering
53 Fool
55 Interlock
57 Morning side dish
60 Have yet to pay
62 On top of that
63 Put on
64 Baseball great Mel
65 Civil War initials

39 REMEMBERING ROCK

Bill Hendricks

ACROSS

1 Science room, for short
4 Michael of tennis
9 Fundamentals
13 "It's Impossible" singer
14 Gulf Coast city
15 Perfume holder
16 Rock Hudson film of '68
19 Rock Hudson film of '51
20 Bandleader Tommy or Jimmy
21 Knight's title
22 *Peer __*
23 Spanish *"chez moi"*
27 Big book
28 Energy
31 Have __ for news
32 Brass-band instrument
33 Panasonic rival
34 Rock Hudson TV series, 1971-76
37 Guys
38 Chopped down
39 Moray catcher
40 Cortes' quest
41 Thumbs-up votes
42 Gets permission for
43 Just __ (minimally)
44 Colonial descendants' grp.
45 Fashion photographer Richard
48 Frequent Rock Hudson costar

53 Hudson film with 48 Across
55 Gait
56 "__ Be There" (Michael Jackson tune)
57 Genesis son
58 Winter glider
59 Party attendee
60 Actress Zadora

DOWN

1 Places
2 Part of AFL
3 Bartlett's cousin
4 Ballparks
5 Spud
6 Fake: Abbr.
7 Navy rank, initially
8 Part of the maintenance staff
9 Stave off
10 Chest protectors
11 Meticulousness
12 Do in
13 Spy org.
17 Mortarboard hanging
18 Sector
22 Spoil
23 Rumba relative
24 Bring down upon oneself
25 Mini-band
26 Warts and all
27 Melodies
28 Magician's word
29 Draw conclusions
30 Fort __, FL
32 Imposed a levy
33 __' Pea (*Popeye* kid)
35 Bomb on stage
36 Actress Dolores
41 Molecule bit
42 "Honest Ed's Auto Land," e.g.
43 Said more
44 Lenient ones
45 Cobras' kin
46 Scaloppine need
47 Suffix of action
48 Lavish attention (on)
49 Trade
50 Figure-skater Thomas
51 Land measure
52 Designer monogram
54 __-TURN (highway sign)

Rich Norris

ACROSS

1 Tiny, in Scotland
4 Rig on the road
8 Shade trees
12 Prom flowers
14 Find innocent
16 Attendance check
17 Black-and-blue mark
18 Region
19 JFK's predecessor
20 Lifts up
21 Basil-based sauce
23 Go no more
25 Part of I.R.S.
27 Video game sites
32 To's opposite
35 Slugger Hank
38 Tabriz native
39 Charge-card system
42 __-trump (bridge bid)
43 Showing no emotion
44 Punch relative
45 Animal that eats tree leaves
47 Model Carol
49 Work the land
51 Put up
55 "Never mind!"
59 Scull propeller
62 Love, to Livy
63 Royal residence
64 Michael J. Fox sitcom
66 Places for bracelets
67 Hides
68 Capone's nemesis

69 Govt. workplace watchdog
70 Fast plane

DOWN

1 Metal leftovers
2 Bruce Willis' ex-wife
3 1888 van Gogh destination
4 Animal pouch
5 "Zounds!"
6 Pinochle holding
7 Spots of land
8 Prefix with lateral
9 San __ Obispo, CA
10 Vapor
11 Fr. holy women
13 Chair parts

14 More than dislike
15 UFO evidence, to some
22 White House room
24 Ballroom dance
26 Cleveland cager, for short
28 "__ you for real?"
29 Infant's word
30 City west of Tulsa
31 Locale
32 Throat clogger?
33 Actor Santoni
34 "Your turn," to a CBer
36 Chorus platform

37 Canadian province: Abbr.
40 Stop __ dime
41 Bush's org., once
46 Mythological trio
48 Slight indication
50 Rapidly, in music
52 Gives off
53 Pigeon coops
54 Rendezvous
55 Stretch across
56 *Citizen* __
57 Types
58 Good buddies
60 Simians
61 Charlie of country music
65 Powerful D.C. lobby

41 TOOT SUITE

Fred Piscop

ACROSS

1 Minor Prophet
5 Rum cakes
10 Actress Ward
14 Actress Virna
15 In plain view
16 Puritan
17 Arthur of tennis
18 TV deputy
20 Japanese beetle, e.g.
22 Clinton's veep
23 Author Follett
24 __ Lopez (chess opening)
25 Bandleader Larry
27 Footballer portrayed by James Caan
33 Musical asset
34 Indonesian island
35 Lux and Ivory
39 And others, in brief
41 Reputations
43 Pianist Peter
44 Spanish mister
46 Is introduced to
48 Burgle
49 Some campaign appearances
52 Computer-screen indicator
55 __ Khan
56 One: Sp.
57 Urgent
60 Ore. peak
64 Pie feature
67 __ la Douce
68 Tropical fruits
69 Sanctum preceder
70 __ off (started golfing)
71 Stair part
72 Hibachi needs
73 Charged particles

DOWN

1 "Too bad!"
2 Catchall category: Abbr.
3 Job-safety org.
4 __ Club (conservation group)
5 Hair holder
6 Actress Gardner
7 Glacier breakaway
8 Florence's river
9 Hi-fi
10 Tanning-lotion letters
11 Soaps star Slezak
12 The Birdman of Alcatraz was one
13 Representative
19 Hollers
21 Mom's sister
26 Hired thug
27 Honey makers
28 Deserve, as a raise
29 Where Farsi is spoken
30 Mosque leaders
31 Hale-Bopp, e.g.
32 Angler's basket
36 Flying word form
37 Stage item
38 Weeps
40 Weather zones
42 Clambake morsels
45 __ Island Red
47 An NCO
50 Of an eye part
51 *Bounty* stop
52 Sleeve ends
53 Dark
54 Khmer __
58 Nevada city
59 Author Ferber
61 Hydrox lookalike
62 Prophetic sign
63 June honorees
65 Recipe meas.
66 Toothpaste type

42 EXPLETIVES SECRETED

Ann Masten

ACROSS

1 Take down __ (demote)
5 "Scramola!"
9 __ Kosher (fit for any rabbi)
14 __ contendere
15 Puerto __
16 Irritate
17 Chances are
20 Dexterity
21 Cheer competitor
22 Sunrise direction
23 Rims
25 Where theories are tested
27 Tinkerbell, e.g.
30 Singer Vikki
31 Dictionary tag: Abbr.
34 *The Good Earth* heroine
35 Blueprint
37 Resource
39 Toon magpies
42 Abdominous
43 Measured amount
44 Narrow in the foot
45 Knight or Kennedy
46 Goatee locale
48 Strawberry of baseball
50 Actress Madlyn
51 Potatoes alternative
52 "I wouldn't do that!"
55 Queue after Q
57 652, to Caesar
61 Some German politicians
64 Woodworker's tool
65 *Omnia vincit __*
66 Greek drink
67 Man of La Mancha
68 Small grid gain
69 Have on

DOWN

1 C __ (cola brand)
2 Unsatisfactory
3 Singer Fitzgerald
4 Tiger Woods' workplace
5 "It's cold!"
6 Shopper's memos
7 It follows Sept. 30
8 Forested areas
9 Main mail bldg.
10 Script elements
11 Light blue
12 Sounds of disapproval
13 Run-through
18 Working hard
19 Cherished
24 __ Le Pew (cartoon skunk)
26 Burns' hillside
27 Not __ (mediocre)
28 First-year cadet
29 Ran
30 Contrapuntal composition
31 Actor Werner
32 Stop, at sea
33 Sneak into second
36 Onetime ballpark promotion
38 Role for Ray Bolger
40 Walesa of Poland
41 Obi-Wan Kenobi, for one
47 Throw hard
49 Like a versatile appliance
50 Big game
51 Bit of gossip
52 Dangerous creepers
53 Bagel middle
54 Open __ of worms
56 Musical motif
58 German physics Nobelist
59 Chichen __
60 "Is You __ Is You Ain't My Baby?"
62 Meteorologist's word form
63 Former fort near Monterey

43 ENGINEER TALK

S.N.

ACROSS

1 Porous gems
6 Letter carrier's burden
10 Actress Nelligan
14 Ignited again
15 __ close to schedule
16 Israeli airline
17 Digresses
20 Pancake pan
21 Hard rubber
22 Have coming
23 Alphabetic trio
24 One of these
27 Compass reading
29 "A guy walks into __ . . ."
33 Tailor's work
34 Talk like Daffy Duck
36 Miss Molly of song
38 State one's views
41 Little laugh
42 Paris airport
43 Prefix for classical
44 Singer Guthrie
45 Ring result
46 Tree beginning
47 Western Indian
49 Pig of films
52 Pricey spice
56 Hermitic
60 Orderly ideas
62 Dry as a desert
63 Deepest Great Lake
64 Like the Mississippi
65 Unadorned
66 Founded: Abbr.
67 Clockmaker Thomas et al.

DOWN

1 Special-interest grps.
2 Cheat at Hide and Seek
3 Word form for "height"
4 Cotton threads
5 Roman robe
6 Towel asset
7 Termite, essentially
8 Stick together
9 Dobie Gillis' buddy
10 *Show Boat* composer
11 Jai __
12 Mediator's must
13 Actress Sommer
18 Iron: Fr.
19 House crawler
24 Greek letter
25 Witch, often
26 Urge forward
28 Frighten
29 __ Baba
30 "April Love" singer
31 French year
32 Patch up a lawn
34 Gettysburg loser
35 Ending for expert
36 $1,000,000, for short
37 Whichever
39 Greek letter
40 Certified, as a will
45 Choral section
46 Unthreatened
47 Coffee brewer
48 "We're Off __ the Wizard"
50 Wood for bats
51 Simpletons
52 Wild guess
53 Irish expletive
54 Impartial
55 Bona __
57 "__ the sun in the morning . . ."
58 "I wouldn't do that!"
59 Express trains: Abbr.
61 Apropos

44 BORDERLINE

Rich Norris

ACROSS

1 Polite form of address
5 Opposite of fem.
9 Flower growing areas
13 USC rival
14 Spotted horse
15 Bluish green
16 Amaze
17 *Jeopardy!* contestant, e.g.
18 Ballerina's skirt
19 The Rockies, for one
22 Wee tykes
24 L.A. Lakers' org.
25 Earl Grey or pekoe
26 Landers or Miller
27 Greenish blue
30 Means of approach
32 Carry with effort
34 Theatre district
36 Hypothetical ape-human connection
40 Lawn gadget
41 Fake
44 Show good manners
47 Cook's condiment
50 Be indebted
51 Before, to a poet
52 Feminine word ending
54 Tooth covering
56 Couldn't decide
60 *The Thin Man* dog

61 Western film
62 Phonograph, for short
65 Smell bad
66 Sarcasm
67 Son of Seth
68 Goofs up
69 Watch over
70 Meal plan

DOWN

1 Bandleader's subj.
2 Do something
3 Foil material
4 Lord's land
5 A little fog
6 Singer Paul
7 Beer mug
8 Heavy-handed sentimentalist
9 Shower option
10 Represent as the same
11 Obligations
12 Spa offerings
14 Kind of violet
20 Family member, familiarly
21 Desert plants
22 Scrooge's complaint
23 Santa __, CA
28 Like the Gobi
29 Dressed to the __
31 Partner of pros
33 Kudrow of *Friends*
35 Taj Mahal site
37 Rome's hill complement

38 Makes certain
39 The Ayatollah
42 Great admiration
43 Director Brooks
44 Cautionary word
45 Pencil end
46 *The Scarlet Letter* character
48 Suspicious (of)
49 Nashville cable sta.
53 Stock unit
55 Was sore
57 Acorn sources
58 School on the Thames
59 Ward (off)
63 Enemy
64 Follower: suff.

45 PLUGGED IN

Rich Norris

ACROSS

1 Sweethearts
5 Conditional phrase
9 Parts of a list
14 Guitarist Clapton
15 Singer Horne
16 Combines, as ingredients
17 Baptism, e.g.
18 Bulletin-board fastener
19 Midler or Davis
20 Running out of time
23 Influential group
24 Spot of paint
25 Brit. fliers
28 Police investigator: Abbr.
29 Make fun of
33 Mystical meeting
35 Splatter catchers
37 Hard to find
38 Means of release for feelings
43 Sitarist Shankar
44 Moves like a mouse
45 Quick drawing
48 Hung on to
49 __ Na Na
52 Always, poetically
53 __ Cruces, NM
55 Rule of conduct
57 Kept up-to-date
62 Threesomes
64 Twist out of shape

65 Therefore
66 Seeps slowly
67 Cupid's Greek counterpart
68 Rich Little, for one
69 Destitute
70 Wet, as morning grass
71 June honorees

DOWN

1 Got the cattle together
2 Baltimore player
3 Dolt
4 Agreeable odor
5 Choir member
6 Do an usher's job
7 Move slowly
8 Made believe
9 Have a drink
10 Stadium level
11 Not from within
12 Bumped into
13 Opposite of NNW
21 Allegro, largo, etc.
22 Existed
26 Land measure
27 Elevation units
30 Gold: Sp.
31 Pros and __
32 Special aptitude
34 They may be liberal
35 Working hard
36 Gin flavoring
38 Gaelic

39 Earn, as money
40 Like some atlases
41 "Alley __!"
42 Say
46 Very stylish
47 Loft material
49 Himalayan guide
50 Like a door
51 Cast members
54 Stitched
56 Tire feature
58 Word after open or pigeon
59 Challenge
60 Boast
61 "__-daisy!"
62 Heavy weight
63 Wade opponent of 1973

46 HOLD EVERYTHING

Norma Steinberg

ACROSS

1 Pants accessory
5 Part of a stair
10 Snakes
14 Opera solo
15 Quitter's word
16 Stubborn beast
17 Nervous wreck
19 Dueling weapon
20 Fall flower
21 Sahara-like
22 Breach of security
23 Vacation spot
25 Corporal's reply
27 Secondhand
29 Nun's garb
32 Liquid conduit
35 Subtlety
39 Keatsian output
40 I: Ger.
41 Office machines
42 Minuscule
43 Gingery drink
44 Words of warning
45 Family group
46 Endures
48 Mexican sandwich
50 Snitch
54 Harass
58 Parts of circles
60 Fifty percent
62 Composer Eubie
63 Source
64 Land near the Mississippi
66 Run in neutral
67 __ a customer

68 Hardens
69 British alphabet enders
70 Troubled
71 Model Macpherson

DOWN

1 Elephant king of kiddie lit
2 Delete
3 Agendas
4 Menu option
5 Boring routine
6 Ancient Peruvian
7 Hair-raising
8 '20s actress Janis
9 Bulrushes

10 Aviatrix Earhart
11 January event
12 Entreaty
13 Car-radio button
18 Goofs
24 Barbershop quartet part
26 "__ only a bird . . ."
28 Hoodwink
30 Think-tank output
31 Numerical ending
32 "Don't touch that __!"
33 Home of the Bruins
34 Wintertime woe

36 Feel poorly
37 Finch's home
38 Elite
41 Expenditure
45 Artistic arrangement
47 Samples
49 "The Georgia Peach"
51 Pulsate
52 He sang "High Noon"
53 Santa's helpers
55 Artist's stand
56 Ability
57 High-strung
58 Calif. neighbor
59 Took the escalator
61 Celebration
65 "Baloney!"

47 GENERALLY SPEAKING

Craig Kasper

ACROSS

1 Nuclear missile's cargo
6 Largest land mass
10 Beside oneself
14 Greyish-brown shade
15 Arctic
16 Silent performer
17 For the most part
19 Not quite round
20 AMA members
21 Detroit footballer
22 New York borough
24 Bandleader Puente
25 Giant-sized
26 Legree et al.
29 Afternoon social event
32 One hundred smackers
33 Schooner's poles
34 Make a knot
35 Permed hairstyle
36 Poetry
37 Talking doll's word
38 Bruce or Pinky
39 Tractor maker John
40 Birthday desserts
41 One's belongings
43 Cathedral cleric
44 Large chasms
45 Like jackhammers
46 Pontius __
48 Star Trek: Deep Space __

49 Dole's grp.
52 Unspoiled place
53 For the most part
56 In addition
57 Demolish
58 Napoleon's fate
59 Actress Harper
60 Related (to)
61 Turn off

DOWN

1 Molecule constituent
2 Musical group
3 Alibis
4 Speedometer letters
5 Direct route
6 "Gesundheit!" preceder
7 In a minute
8 Under the weather
9 Sufficient
10 One-celled animal
11 Approximately
12 Neighbor of Yemen
13 Some toothpastes
18 Funny folk
23 Baseball officials
24 Oz pooch
25 Outlaw James
26 Head part
27 Draw a conclusion
28 Approximately
29 Linger
30 Race statistics
31 Bread ingredient
33 Track competitions
36 Back bone
37 Manor cleaner
39 Sure-handed
40 More nasty
42 Home instruments
43 Frog's hangout
45 Bedsheet fabric
46 Boggy soil
47 Not in use
48 Indiana Jones foe
49 Hold onto
50 Stare at
51 Banana covering
54 Shoot the breeze
55 Lumberjack's need

48 STRETCHING THE TRUTH

Fred Piscop

ACROSS

1 Slot inserts
5 Piglike animal
10 Troubadour
14 Hershey's Syrup rival
15 Ease up
16 Toledo's lake
17 Gaucho's weapon
18 Gogol's __ *Bulba*
19 *Glamour* rival
20 Contrabass
22 Make a crease
23 Sharp instruments
24 Dunces
26 Gets thinner
30 Independence-gainer of 1991
34 __ glance (quickly)
37 Modern messages
39 Advertising lights
40 Brown-bagger's lunch, perhaps
43 Santa __, CA
44 Brazilian dance
45 Daniel __-Lewis
46 Skedaddles
48 Inclined
50 In apple-pie order
52 Grouch
56 Fake coin
59 Ranch sleeping quarters
63 Hired car
64 Russian writer Bonner
65 Big butte
66 It flows through Stratford
67 66 Across, for one
68 Green shot
69 Silents star Theda
70 Bullock film
71 Therapeutic spots

DOWN

1 *Miami Vice* role
2 Circa
3 Tummy
4 Plays for time
5 Jacques of French comedy
6 ". . . no such thing as __ boy"
7 Colleague, out west
8 Novelist Calvino
9 Close the envelope again
10 Meal in a can
11 First name in folk singing
12 Small brook
13 Monopoly card
21 Computer-data identifier
25 Triple-time dance
27 __ *Mine* (George Harrison book)
28 Hitter of 660 homers
29 Rug fiber
31 Null's partner
32 Andean of old
33 Pallid
34 The basics
35 Bath powder
36 Banned apple spray
38 Glittery fabric
41 Citrus drink
42 Hoop grp.
47 Cavalry weapons
49 Outdoes
51 Tiny Tim's favorite flower
53 Exhaust
54 Socialite Perle
55 H.S. juniors' exams
56 Wild guess
57 Vesuvius outflow
58 Wife, in legalese
60 Glacial snow
61 Place for a pants patch
62 Like some cider

49 UNDER CONTRACT

Norma Steinberg

ACROSS

1 Nautical cry
5 Ugly Duckling, eventually
9 Nuke, as leftovers
12 Relocate
13 He hit 61 homers in '61
15 Ashen
16 Spin doctor
18 Wight, for one
19 __ Salvador
20 Chief exec.
21 Once-a-year
23 Cliques
24 Gator's kin
25 Strut
28 Skillful ones
32 Salesperson
33 Jerk
34 Front of a ship
35 Sitarist Shankar
36 Notebook contents
37 Raison d'__
38 Prayer response
39 Roman poet
40 Fairy-tale figure
41 Entree choice
43 Easter hat
44 Sentence fragment
45 Like venison
46 Hamilton or Harrison
49 French father
50 Poem
53 __ mater
54 Accordion
57 Cry
58 Pachyderm's teeth
59 "__ lay me down to sleep . . ."
60 Barbie's boyfriend
61 Aide: Abbr.
62 Fender flaw

DOWN

1 Bandstand equipment
2 Israeli dance
3 Pizzeria appliance
4 "Uh huh!"
5 Wise guy
6 Salary
7 War god
8 Diarist Anaïs
9 Actress Pitts
10 __ breve
11 Fruit covering
14 Race official
15 Miser
17 Talk
22 Negative votes
23 Plastic packaging
24 Made do
25 Throw out
26 Memorable mission
27 Become separated
28 Words to a hitchhiker
29 English playwright
30 The Velvet Fog
31 Sugary
33 Biblical king
36 Neediest
40 *Addams Family* name
42 Fireplace filler
43 Least adorned
45 Nerds
46 Rubberneck
47 Robt. __
48 Augury
49 "__ in Boots"
50 Woodwind
51 Duck feathers
52 Way out
55 Sine __ non
56 Conclude

50 MEASURING UP

Lee Weaver

ACROSS

1 Comic Carvey
5 Fragrant wood
10 Long way off
14 Unrefined metals
15 Old saying
16 Bishop of Rome
17 Angler's equipment
19 Work as a model
20 Musical notes
21 One's manner
22 Tried to reduce
24 Hourglass contents
25 Not against the rules
26 Journey
29 Showing respect for
32 Egg-shaped
33 Stair part
34 __ long way (last)
35 Exhaust
36 Hardened
37 Those over there
38 Goal
39 Hopeless case
40 Ownership document
41 One with doubts
43 Suitable for evening wear
44 Licorice-like flavoring
45 Data-speed unit
46 Money in Spain
48 Send a package
49 Yellow Pages entries
52 Singer James
53 Shoelace tie
56 Small bills
57 Showy display
58 Gumbo ingredient
59 __ a one (none)
60 Oscar-winner Field
61 Moby Dick seeker

DOWN

1 Remove, as a hat
2 Diva's big moment
3 Scottish loch
4 Hibachi residue
5 Wolf or fox
6 Trimmed the lawn
7 Repair a sock
8 In the past
9 Blushed
10 Show up
11 Stage illumination
12 Church recess
13 Cattail, e.g.
18 Mirror reflection
23 Composer Stravinsky
24 Fill to the brim
25 Also-ran
26 Took part in the election
27 Sheepish?
28 Railroad superintendent
29 Backpacker, e.g.
30 Yuletide songs
31 Tasting like venison
33 Indian queen
36 Prom-time posies
37 Deadlocked
39 True __ (Wayne movie)
40 Factually
42 On pins and needles
43 Delicately pretty
45 Run-of-the-mill
46 Unskilled laborer
47 European volcano
48 Teen's hangout
49 Egyptian cross
50 Mrs. Copperfield
51 Wild guess
54 Magnavox competitor
55 Campground initials

HOME SWEET HOME

Rich Norris

ACROSS

1 Performance
5 Auntie of Broadway
9 Snake with a hood
14 Bluefin, for one
15 Not home
16 An archangel
17 Came down
18 Ivy League school
19 Cooking appliance
20 Salad topping
23 Cabbage unit
24 Slip a __ (err)
25 Cheap and showy
28 Bikini part
30 Used needle and thread
34 Figure of speech
35 Diets, with "down"
37 By way of
38 Protest formally
41 Before, to a poet
42 Extends across
43 Pass, as a law
44 Family rooms
46 Also
47 Small bus
48 Railroad unit
50 Biblical trio
51 Milk product
57 Lagoon surrounder
59 Vichyssoise ingredient
60 Theater level
61 Bamboo-eating mammal
62 "¿Que __?"
63 Region
64 Lock of hair
65 Pitcher Hershiser
66 Unpleasant situation

DOWN

1 Sky sight
2 Waikiki dance
3 Getting __ years
4 House guardian
5 Word of distress
6 Oscar or Edgar
7 Oscar or Edgar
8 Peepers
9 Collector's item
10 Bornean apes
11 Harry Lillis Crosby
12 Rule, for short
13 Tap choice
21 Mercury, to the Greeks
22 Troublemaker
25 Like some floors
26 Admire greatly
27 Make broader
28 Fair-haired fellow
29 Canyon borders
31 French spa
32 Flinch
33 Well-dressed
35 Examine carefully
36 Winter vehicle
39 Split up
40 1862 battle site
45 Gives a dressing-down
47 *The Day of the __*
49 Cartographer's project
50 Reagan Cabinet member
51 Ice-cream holder
52 Kal Kan rival
53 Equipment
54 Ireland, to the Irish
55 Goes out with
56 Memorable times
57 Fitting
58 Road covering

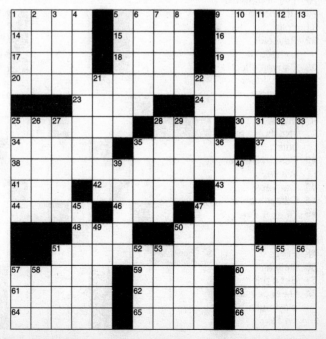

52 SMALL FRY

Sally Stein

ACROSS

1 Rooting section
5 Old Russian ruler
9 Colors crudely
14 Iridescent gem
15 "Pay __ never-mind!"
16 Arctic structure
17 Give or take a few
18 "Give a __ horse he can ride"
19 Slammin' Sam
20 Juvenile menace of comics
23 Shrewd
24 Give it __ (go for it)
25 *The Hustler* star
29 TV interference
30 Hog home
31 Yoko __
32 Reynolds competitor
35 Canyon effect
37 Hill builders
38 Nightgown wearer of rhyme
41 "No ifs, __ or buts!"
42 Peace Nobelist Wiesel
43 Careless
44 Citizen's suffix
45 "It __ a Very Good Year"
46 Melt
48 Flings
50 Dirty air
51 Set a price
54 He once had a playhouse on TV

57 *"10"* star
60 Word form for "eye"
61 Until
62 Any way
63 Golden Spike state
64 Gradual
65 Macho
66 Metric pound
67 Cacklers

DOWN

1 See 2 Down
2 With 1 Down, tricksters' big day
3 Snide
4 Pigeonhole
5 "A __ be born . . ."
6 Where flights can be found
7 Irk
8 Path
9 Entertainment conglomerate
10 Nixon's first V.P.
11 Ending for mod or nod
12 Feathery scarf
13 Lay down the lawn
21 Polynesian porch
22 Under protection
26 Order members
27 Legislative opponents
28 Intrusive
29 Scatters seed
30 Steel-mill output

32 Be in store for
33 Slow tempo
34 Gives up
36 XVII x VI
37 From the top
39 Hire
40 P.R. man's concern
45 Like some newspapers
47 Santa's sound
49 Length of time
50 Numerical prefix
51 Adequate
52 Squelched
53 "The Shadow __"
55 *The Winds of War* author
56 Charge
57 Stop up
58 LAX stat
59 Skedaddled

53 ERIN GO BRAGH

John Leavy

ACROSS
1 Transfixed
5 Biblical king
10 River floater
14 Manipulator
15 Greek-salad item
16 __ Bator, Mongolia
17 Comic Dunn
18 Early evening
19 Actor Brad
20 James Joyce masterpiece
23 Waterfront sight
24 Tinted
25 Shot to pieces
28 Coolly polite
31 *La Bamba* star Morales
32 Perfect embodiment
34 Itsy-bitsy
37 Tropical sitcom
40 *Casablanca* pianist
41 Pure as the driven snow
42 "This shouldn't happen to __!"
43 "It __ Be You"
44 Too big
45 Any minute now
47 Chanteuse Vikki
49 1917 song
55 Solemn ceremony
56 Suspect's excuse
57 Profound
59 Pub orders
60 Half-hearted
61 Actor Sharif
62 Rock singer Joan
63 Act segment
64 Western star Calhoun

DOWN
1 Hosiery snag
2 Ever since
3 Persian fairy
4 Cool as a cucumber
5 Biblical prophet
6 Gray poem
7 Racehorse __ Ridge
8 Major appliance
9 Family rooms
10 Gender-bending singer
11 Identical
12 Predestined
13 Explosive substance
21 Cashew, e.g.
22 Mechanical hums
25 Large barrels
26 Largest continent
27 Tropical tree
28 Poem division
29 __ *Wonderful Life*
30 Colorado ski resort
32 Matured
33 Massive
34 Walk through water
35 Hazzard County deputy
36 Precipice
38 Donald's first
39 Canadian peninsula
43 Straight-shooting
44 Heavenly body
45 Say "cheese"
46 Group of eight
47 Log structure
48 "All kidding __ . . ."
50 Tennis star Wilander
51 Actor Guinness
52 Ready for harvesting
53 Skipper of the *Nautilus*
54 Cherished
55 British rule in India
58 Snoop

54 ON LINE

Rich Norris

ACROSS

1 Mideast gulf
6 Some ballpoints
10 Hit the mall
14 Moons, in Madrid
15 Feel sore
16 Angelic aura
17 Clothes-dryer insert
19 Early automaker
20 Moves toward
22 Be deceitful
23 Goes back to zero
26 Banged into
28 Lodge members
29 Hardy heroine
33 Word form for "earth"
34 British brew
35 Einsteins
36 Copier additive
39 Sebastian Coe, for one
41 PC key
42 Jungian principle
43 Take care of
44 Trolley sound
46 Vietnamese New Year
47 Dancing-shoe attachment
48 Beginner
49 Adam and Hoss, to Ben
50 Bad temper
53 Pageboy, for one
55 Writer Fleming
56 9 to 5, e.g.
60 Greek goddess of victory
62 Crispy snack
66 Mr. Kadiddle-hopper
67 Afghanistan neighbor
68 Path
69 Attention getters
70 Coming-out VIPs
71 Barbecue leftover

DOWN

1 Without exception
2 On the __ vive
3 Columnist Landers
4 Enjoys the tub
5 Positive element
6 Poet
7 Cool dessert
8 Restaurant VIP
9 Spanish mister
10 "__ nuff!"
11 High-school sentinel
12 Blast from the past
13 Had portraits taken
18 Social stratum
21 Diverse
23 Lots of paper
24 J.R.'s mother
25 Multidoor opener
27 "Are you putting __?"
30 Make laws
31 Featherbrained
32 Shankar's strings
35 Sought clumsily
37 Make changes
38 *Midnight Cowboy* role
40 List extender
45 Pitcher's dream game
49 *Friends*, for one
50 Piece of cake
51 __ Selassie
52 Fast
54 Ere
57 Olden days
58 Wild attempt
59 Actor Conried
61 Printer's measures
63 Center of activity
64 Descendant: Suff.
65 According to

55 ENGLISH 101

Rich Norris

ACROSS
1 Study feverishly
5 Wood that moths hate
10 Con game
14 Go here and there
15 Angry
16 "Sorry I spilled that!"
17 Ice cream additive
18 Wanderer
19 Hawaiian strings, for short
20 Corporate communication
23 Hunting dog
24 Eye protector
25 Piece of postage
28 Moments of forgetfulness
32 Hydrocarbon suffix
35 "The Red Planet"
37 Proportional expression
38 Believes without questioning
42 __ a customer
43 Wise__owl
44 Round veggie
45 Brute strength
47 Give encouragement to
50 Eastern European dance
52 Freezes, as a windshield
56 Capone served one
60 One of the Aldas
61 The squiggle in *señor*
62 Portal

63 Warbled
64 Public persona
65 Inventor Rubik
66 Refreshes a stamp pad
67 Frolic
68 Collision consequence

DOWN
1 Seafood selections
2 Scoundrel
3 29 Down, at sea
4 Is deserving of
5 Wide-screen film process
6 Son of Aphrodite
7 River blockers
8 In any way
9 Card-on-the-floor result
10 Lefty

11 Pepsi alternative
12 Mimic
13 SASE enclosures
21 Circus safety device
22 Russian rulers
26 __ Hari
27 Text in paragraphs
29 "Whoa!"
30 Ireland
31 Scotch partner
32 Nuclear-energy source
33 Half of Mork's sign-off
34 Supplements, with "out"
36 Unexpected problem
39 Artist's creations

40 Goes it alone
41 Motorman
46 Sensuous
48 Halloween's mo.
49 Couldn't do without
51 Jungian principle
53 Night noise
54 '95 NCAA women's basketball champs
55 Upstart candidate of '92
56 Make arrangements
57 Military level
58 Mild penalty
59 Barely beat
60 "It's just __ thought!"

56 GONE FISHING

Brendan Quigley

AROSS

1 Dutch cheese
5 *Star Wars* character
9 Puppy
14 City in Peru
15 Midterm or final
16 Beach takealong
17 Language learning system
20 "Against a thing," in law
21 Abrasive particles
22 Prefix for picker
23 Halloween attire
26 Stuffed oneself
28 Controversial Presidential option
32 Attorneys' grp.
33 Unaccompanied
34 Moves like the Blob
38 Soil fertilizer
40 *Look Homeward, Angel* author
43 Cancel, as an article
44 Comic Richard
46 Change for a twenty
48 Dead heat
49 Low perspective
53 Legendary siren
56 Information
57 "What a good boy __"
58 Gives a hand to
60 Nonsensical
64 Math-checking procedure
68 Work flour

69 Tickle-Me doll
70 Cereal sound
71 Hole in your head
72 Precisely
73 Antler

DOWN

1 Primary grades, for short
2 Singer Celine
3 Italian love
4 "Don't __ Over" (Warwick tune)
5 A Beverly Hillbilly
6 Prefix meaning "outer"
7 "Phooey!"
8 Ad-lib comedy
9 Corresponded with
10 With 59 Down, *Star Wars* character
11 Minnesota town
12 Permitted by law
13 Correspondence, in Caen
18 Correspondence via computers
19 Bee shelter
24 Put away
25 Gambling game
27 Chess piece
28 Genie's home
29 Girder
30 Not a one
31 Defrosts
35 Tubular pasta
36 Writer Wiesel
37 Did in
39 Actor Rob

41 Farm animals' dinner
42 Irish singer
45 Tums competitor
47 Harden
50 Jockey's brake
51 Reduced-size replica
52 Disappear
53 Doesn't have
54 Certain Arab
55 Gone up
59 See 10 Down
61 Part of A.D.
62 Within reach
63 Sports cable channel
65 Greek letter
66 Thurman of *Batman & Robin*
67 Kiddie

57 TABLE SETTING

Rich Norris

ACROSS

1 Hive hubbub
5 Relieved sighs
8 Multiplex offerings
14 Dueling sword
15 __ tai (rum cocktail)
16 American Leaguer
17 Pasadena arena
19 "__ the U.S.A." (Springsteen song)
20 Potent explosive
21 Scottish hillside
22 Former Yugoslav leader
23 Extraterrestrial carrier
27 Skater's jump
30 Stalactite shape
31 Esprit de corps
34 Airline to Jerusalem
35 Some M.I.T. grads
38 NBC's California headquarters
40 Wash-and-wear
42 "__ about time!"
43 Take seriously
45 Fakes, as illness
46 *Silkwood* actress
48 Novgorod negative
49 Stylish dresser
54 Voice above tenor
55 Dinghy needs
56 Music players at weddings
59 Billiard shots
62 Biennial pro golf competition
64 Writes to, via modem
65 Chinese principle
66 Luke Skywalker's mentor
67 Local resident, to a collegian
68 Narrow body of water: Abbr.
69 Extremes

DOWN

1 Actor Lahr
2 "Once __ a time . . ."
3 Enthusiasm
4 Last letter
5 Writer Cleveland __
6 Pineapple source
7 "Hush!"
8 Disorderly group
9 Pizarro's quest
10 Moral excellence
11 Greek column type
12 Upper crust
13 Mister, in Madrid
18 Crude-oil unit: Abbr.
23 Bodybuilder's bane
24 __ the lily
25 Winter neckwear
26 Kate's TV companion
27 Prefix meaning "both"
28 Cross off
29 Is mistaken
32 Christine of *Chicago Hope*
33 January, in Spain
35 Tense
36 Sea eagle
37 Part of CBS
39 Penetrating, as insight
41 Long (for)
44 Sends out of the country
46 Sure winner
47 Perform frivolously
49 Diamond surface
50 1836 siege site
51 Sipper's need
52 Intensity
53 Mao __-tung
56 Raid competitor
57 Wynonna or Naomi
58 Health resorts
60 11th-century date
61 U-turn from NNW
63 Pumpernickel alternative

58 THE HARD STUFF

Norma Steinberg

ACROSS
1 Voodoo amulet
5 Rover's pal
9 Very loud, in music
12 Swear
13 Not moving
15 Seethe
16 Bakery buy
18 Stare at
19 Tundra animal
20 __ even keel
21 "We are not __!"
23 Gets free (of)
24 Second son
25 Party handouts
28 Wield
32 Linda Lavin role
33 Nixon chief of staff
34 Author Ferber
35 Bottle part
36 Scouting outings
37 Civil unrest
38 Seize
39 Some poems
40 Put on a pedestal
41 Mightier
43 Covered with metal
44 Drags
45 Part of a hand
46 Meditation phrase
49 Statistics
50 Ring victories
53 Margarine
54 Megalithic monument
57 Flower part
58 Sanctuary
59 Quayle's successor
60 Bricklayer's implement
61 Sash
62 Was obligated to

DOWN
1 Musical Auntie
2 Elliptical
3 Soda-fountain worker
4 Sphere
5 Villains
6 Ancient Peruvians
7 College official
8 Mork's home
9 Mists
10 Arrange alphabetically
11 Ran away
14 Pekoe holders
15 Huge Nevada structure
17 River at Orléans
22 A Few Good __
23 Absolute lowest
24 Zodiac sign
25 Dracula's teeth
26 Bright-eyed
27 Clergyman
28 Singer Anita
29 Knucklehead
30 Sleeper's sound
31 Despised
33 Puts out of sight
36 "Baloney!"
40 Koran creator
42 ". . . __ gloom of night . . ."
43 Inventor's protection
45 Committee
46 Slam-dance
47 Voice range
48 Prerequisite
49 Peacenik
50 Have memorized
51 Monster
52 Planter's purchase
55 Typewriter key
56 Sense of self

59 WELL-DRESSED

Rich Norris

ACROSS

1 London area
4 More competent
9 __ Bill (legendary cowboy)
14 Bobby of hockey
15 Actress Sonia
16 Precise
17 "__ we there yet?"
18 Vietnam's capital
19 Takes it easy
20 Made bad investments
23 Communion table
24 Sunrise direction
25 Scores in overtime, e.g.
32 Health resort
35 Moran of *Happy Days*
36 Daffy or Donald
37 Bagel filler
38 Great pleasure
42 Speller's competition
43 Oil cartel
45 Cab passenger
46 Program interruptions
47 Not at all sportsmanlike
52 Siamese
53 Clear the blackboard
57 Is boss at home
61 Spin
63 "__ evil, hear . . ."
64 Xenon, e.g.
65 Scary
66 Fielder's misplay
67 Holiday precursor
68 Joyce Kilmer poem
69 Accomplished, old-style
70 Critic Reed

DOWN

1 Australian marsupial
2 Swashbuckling actor Flynn
3 Seize forcibly
4 More than disliked
5 Healthful cereal grain
6 Country byway
7 Selves
8 Brings up, as an issue
9 Cease to exist
10 Made a notable effort
11 __ off (set sail)
12 Fall mo.
13 Holy men: Abbr.
21 Actor Hunter
22 Headgear
26 "Able was I __ . . ."
27 Be indisposed
28 Table setting item
29 Marching band instrument
30 Topped off the cake
31 Squeezes (out), as a living
32 Messy one
33 Poet Alexander
34 Skater's jump
39 Gift of the talkative
40 Charlemagne's reign: Abbr.
41 Move via mental processes
44 Exclusive group
48 Large sea mammals
49 Sailor
50 Showed displeasure publicly
51 Singer's syllable
54 Fury
55 Barrel component
56 English county
57 Telegram
58 Hatcher of *Lois & Clark*
59 Cattle cluster
60 Grandson of Adam
61 Drenched
62 That girl

60 CHIMING IN

Bob Lubbers

ACROSS

1 Possessive pronoun
6 Baby's word
10 Lost buoyancy
14 Singer Lena
15 Rara __
16 Pennsylvania port
17 Grand productions
18 With tolerance
20 Graduation keepsakes
22 Employs
23 Ladies' men
27 Disdains
31 Burro
33 Consume
34 Carrying a rifle
35 Architect Saarinen
37 "__ Lama Ding Dong"
38 Outbursts of amusement
41 Small horse
42 "Satin __" (Ellington tune)
43 Della or Pee Wee
44 Actor Wallach
45 At any time, to a poet
46 Card game
47 Alarm button
49 "Hallelujah!"
51 Certain travel costs
57 Cookouts
60 Sandy expanse
62 Fencer's sword
63 Author Ferber
64 Hawaiian veranda
65 Heavy burden
66 Hardens
67 Waxed cheeses

DOWN

1 Common title-starter
2 Jumps on one foot
3 Actor Stoltz
4 Foot division
5 Echoes
6 *Pretty Baby* director
7 States strongly
8 Short skirt
9 B __ "boy"
10 Logic
11 Comic actor Carney
12 Zilch
13 Islet
19 Urges (on)
21 CIA predecessor
24 Less mussed
25 Most docile
26 Ogles, with "at"
27 Demolition expert
28 Spicy cuisine
29 Muscat residents
30 Depend (on)
31 Asian sea
32 Former French coin
35 Get an __ effort
36 Building addition
37 Actress Perlman
39 Lyric poem
40 Winter Olympics site of '68
45 Raison d'__
46 All __ up (steamed)
48 Abated
49 Ten-percenter
50 Some flattops
52 Summer dessert
53 Weekend rancher
54 Heavy metal
55 Turner or Cantrell
56 Con game
57 __ canto (singing style)
58 Mil. address
59 Actor Stephen
61 Part of HRH

61 LET ME IN!

Rich Norris

ACROSS
1 High cards
5 Wilkes-___, PA
10 With competence
14 No different
15 Blunted swords
16 Fence attachment
17 Wander aimlessly
19 Comes to a finish
20 Skipped a dance
21 Mattress part
23 Ivan of tennis
24 Shrewd
27 Anonymous John
28 Glass sheet
30 Greek letter
31 Runs easily
34 Spree
35 *Beverly Hillbillies* character
36 Tennis-shirt name
37 Plucky courage
38 Canine command
39 Singer Rawls
40 Roman Empire language
41 Serious
42 Actress Jillian
43 North Carolina county
44 Pub selection
45 Actor Sir ___ Hardwicke
47 Warehouse containers
50 Ocean growths
53 Wading birds
55 To-do
57 Informal chat
59 Kid's transport
60 Decorate
61 Actress Spelling
62 March 15th, e.g.
63 Went after
64 Dance component

DOWN
1 Pops a question
2 Artificial waterway
3 Overact
4 Showed support for
5 One of the Fab Four
6 Police alert, briefly
7 Classic cars
8 Enlist again
9 Alienate
10 55 Down employee
11 Extraordinary performance
12 Inc., in Ipswich
13 "Absolutely!"
18 Acclaim
22 "That's clear now!"
25 Unifying idea
26 Type of duck
28 Mischievous elf
29 Has ___ with (knows well)
31 Reddish purple
32 Endangered atmospheric layer
33 Dessert choice
34 The two
37 Eyelash makeup
38 Achieves detente
40 Animal's home
41 Atlantic City machines
44 Attendance-book notation
46 Lariats
48 *The Waste Land* poet
49 Mall unit
51 Work at the warehouse
52 Dick and Jane's dog
54 Cut a little
55 Govt. detective agcy.
56 Container cover
58 Madrid Mrs.

62 GONNA FLY NOW

John Leavy

ACROSS

1 A Baldwin brother
5 Love god
9 Beseeched
13 Chutzpah
14 Former Egyptian president
16 Civil-rights activist Parks
17 Austen masterpiece
18 Superman's dressing room
20 Not so dull, as clothes
22 Montgomery's WWII foe
23 Chef Graham
24 Co-ed college since 1997
25 Coach Knute
28 German greeting
29 Tiger Woods' org.
32 Marsh bird
33 Retail outlet
34 Guitarist Lofgren
35 Spaceman Shepard
36 Wake up
37 Novelist Hunter
38 Fender bender
39 Model Macpherson
40 Took an oath
41 Wind dir.
42 Parimutuel concern
43 Bandleader Lanin
44 Pig's place
45 Bathday cake
46 Actress Andress

50 Inconsistent
54 Superman's home
56 Cougar
57 Electrical connector
58 Make happy
59 Gouda alternative
60 "Auld Lang __"
61 Neck and neck
62 Philosopher Descartes

DOWN

1 Matures
2 Genie's home
3 Ticklish Muppet
4 Superman's secret identity
5 Aim high
6 *Politically Incorrect* host
7 Polecat's defense
8 Took off
9 Spring fling
10 Weaver's need
11 Spanish compass point
12 Author Roald
15 White ant
19 Seethe
21 Nomad's house
24 Poetry
25 Cracks the books
26 Stares at
27 Winch
28 Carries
29 Swivel
30 Menacing look
31 *Lou Grant* star

33 Hackneyed
34 4 Down's workplace
36 Bureaucratic delay
40 Char
42 Ibsen's home
43 Undo, as ropes
45 Ill will
46 Diamond authorities
47 Count (on)
48 Daze
49 Powerful impulse
50 Pole, for instance
51 Guy, in surferese
52 Mrs. David Bowie
53 Showed up
55 Bullring cheer

WHERE YOU LIVE

Rich Norris

ACROSS

1 CD precursors
4 __ *Gotta Have It* (Spike Lee film)
8 *Yankee Doodle Dandy* Oscar-winner
14 Boxer Muhammad
15 Grotto
16 Used one's key
17 Fellow
18 *Roots* writer Haley
19 Folks like Scrooge
20 Perky 1994 USA skiing medalist
23 Stair segment
24 Have lunch
25 Official proceedings
29 Celebrate with enthusiasm
34 Superficial amounts
37 Lukewarm
38 Mrs. Nixon
39 "Are you a man __ mouse?"
40 Sound of relief
42 Chemical suffix
43 Composer Berg
45 Astronomical events
47 Sanctified condition
50 Yucatan native
51 Wrinkle-nosed dog
52 Singer Diana
56 Dwight Yoakam's field
61 Grown-ups
64 Buckeye State
65 Altar phrase
66 Phoenician, for one
67 Aug. follower
68 "Hold On Tight" rock group
69 African mammals
70 Return-mail enclosure: Abbr.
71 Account exec

DOWN

1 Reading lights
2 Braid of hair
3 As of
4 Strikebreaker
5 Saintly headgear
6 Nights before
7 Small music groups
8 *The Iceman* __
9 ". . . baked in __"
10 Be pregnant
11 Pilot's heading: Abbr.
12 Poetic adverb
13 Gridiron distances: Abbr.
21 CEO's calendar entry
22 Tell (on)
26 Manages somehow
27 Strong cord
28 Lake Titicaca's range
30 Show penitence
31 Occupational suffix
32 Powerful D.C. lobby
33 Value system
34 Burst of activity
35 Island near Sicily
36 In check
40 Not this direction: Abbr.
41 In the style of
44 Rather quickly
45 Picnic competition
46 Lima's country
48 Compositions
49 Enjoyment
53 Wickerwork material
54 Move sideways
55 Ice-cream unit
57 Director Preminger
58 Actress Perlman
59 Kennel sounds
60 Dust speck
61 Fireplace residue
62 "*Agnus* __"
63 Ref's cousin

64 THE WILD BUNCH

Lee Weaver

ACROSS

1 Golf-course stats
5 Detective work
9 Big-band instruments
14 Actor Guinness
15 Poems of praise
16 Wide awake
17 Space shuttle grp.
18 __ avis
19 Mirror reflection
20 Little Bighorn chief
23 Feel remorse
24 Observe
25 Thrown in a high arc
27 Baltic Sea nation
31 One who flies high
33 Operatic solos
34 Camera filler
35 Swindles
38 Finds fault
39 Hägar the Horrible's wife
40 High wind
41 Vigoda and Fortas
42 Singer Fitzgerald
43 Discussion group
44 Something scarce
46 ". . . far beyond those of __ men"
47 Cried noisily
49 Animation unit
50 July sign
51 *Spin City* star

58 Notched, as a leaf
60 Sound from a goose
61 BMW competitor
62 Helped out
63 Cain's brother
64 "I've __ had!"
65 Peevish
66 Too inquisitive
67 Smelting residue

DOWN

1 Kitchen needs
2 Jai __
3 Take it easy
4 Chasing-away word
5 Eye part
6 Old saying
7 Belgrade resident
8 Birthright seller
9 Suit maker
10 Einstein's birthplace
11 Longtime Alabama coach
12 Take the other side
13 War horse
21 Egyptian goddess
22 Andes beast
26 Nonchooser, it's said
27 Actress Turner
28 King Hussein, for one
29 Athlete in the news
30 Feudal tenant
31 Inane
32 Gymnast Korbut

34 Hat material
36 Entreaty
37 Deal in
39 Swiss miss
43 Public-opinion barometer
45 Cure-all
46 Submissively
47 Sheep sound
48 Eagle's nest
49 Walking sticks
52 Sleuth Charlie
53 "King of the road"
54 Fighter's punches
55 Gas or oil
56 Concert halls
57 Word on a school-zone sign
59 Complete collection

65 FOR CRYIN' OUT LOUD

Norma Steinberg

ACROSS

1 Poisonous snakes
5 Clay brick
10 Fool
14 Bloke
15 Memorize
16 "This can't be!"
17 Cry at the Forum
19 Of low quality
20 Bert's pal
21 Puerto __
22 "Well, __ that special!"
23 Pre-photocopier copies
25 Choose
27 Secondhand
29 Cinders
32 Envelope part
35 Views from the mountain top
39 Tundra animal
40 __ Abner
41 Most submissive
42 Slugger's stat
43 Moray
44 Coordinated
45 __ over heels
46 Don of *Get Smart*
48 Muscle condition
50 Turned into
54 Dutch flowers
58 Trudge
60 Force
62 Singer Shore
63 Become well
64 Newsboy's cry
66 About

67 Danger
68 Composer Satie
69 Lord's mate
70 Rendezvous
71 Fair to middlin'

DOWN

1 Pined (for)
2 Ventriloquist Lewis
3 Wall covering
4 Separated
5 __ carte
6 Bambi, e.g.
7 Watering hole
8 Reinforce
9 Sign up
10 Agenda items
11 Knock response

12 A part of
13 Legal wrong
18 Chief execs.
24 __ *Days in May*
26 The Orient
28 Winds down
30 One of Napoleon's homes
31 Slide, as on ice
32 Dog's bane
33 Perjured oneself
34 Conductor's cry
36 The limit, sometimes
37 Bivouac shelter
38 English racing site

41 This and that: Abbr.
45 Spirals
47 Series of songs
49 Hosiery shade
51 Skillful
52 Fraternity party
53 Way in
55 Emcee's speech
56 Helen's abductor
57 Military hat
58 Collins or Silvers
59 Actress Olin
61 Speaker of baseball
65 Height: Abbr.

66 ARTISTIC LICENSE

Patrick Jordan

ACROSS

1. Combine
6. One talking while trucking
10. Colossal, as a film
14. Sound dubber's concern
15. River of Florence
16. Sugar source
17. Create a composition of cushions?
19. Give a job to
20. Lott and colleagues
21. Makes amends
23. "... man __ mouse?"
24. Say "Howdy!" to
25. Shutterbug's need
29. Paneled wall lining
32. Aromas
33. Disconcerted
34. Weeder's need
35. Liver secretion
36. Poker pair
37. Singer Minnelli
38. Stop-sign shade
39. Removed, to a proofreader
40. Deals with a dilemma
41. Aegis
43. Hairstyling foam
44. '96 White House aspirant
45. Sigma follower
46. Like the Ark
48. Athenian philosopher
53. Podded vegetable
54. Create a study in soda sippers?
56. Nothing: Fr.
57. Winter Olympics event
58. He bugs Bugs
59. Bird's home
60. Once around the sun
61. Active folks

DOWN

1. Low voice
2. Gospel writer
3. Genesis locale
4. Silents star Naldi
5. Medicos
6. Film director Frank
7. Bikini parts
8. Bring to a halt
9. Prayer beads
10. Radar signals
11. Create a still life with salty snacks?
12. Concerning
13. Middling grades
18. Israeli dance
22. Take care of
24. Looked longingly
25. African snake
26. Parting word
27. Create embryonic fern figurines?
28. Before, to Burns
29. Buffs the floor
30. Moves like molasses
31. Annoy playfully
33. Cut the bones out
36. "After that ..."
37. Comical Costello
39. Calamitous
40. Went a-wooing
42. Intellectual showoff
43. Some apples
45. Pisa attraction
46. Had on
47. *Grapes of Wrath* figure
48. Heroic tale
49. Guthrie of folk fame
50. Manageable
51. Water pitcher
52. Estonia and Latvia, before 1991: Abbr.
55. Feel sorry about

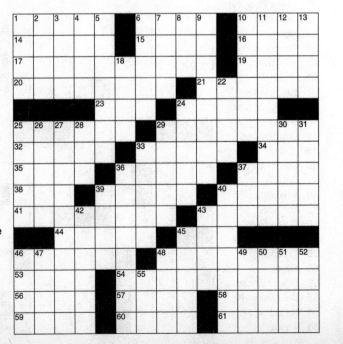

67 HIGHMINDED

Rich Norris

ACROSS

1 Until now
6 Sandbox accessory
10 Rapid
14 Put up with
15 Writer Bombeck
16 Kal Kan rival
17 Prominent hairline feature
19 Story teller
20 Word form for "recent"
21 Glacial epoch
22 Penny
23 Sold-out sign letters
24 Sunday speeches
26 Movie follow-ups
30 Moral violation
31 Egg cell
32 Medicos
35 Felt sore
39 Paper quantity
40 Inner selves
42 Hard to find
43 "Take a chance!"
45 Orderly
46 Moran of *Happy Days*
47 Put to good use
49 Chambermaid's need
51 Sort of warm
55 Court divider
56 Actress Turner
57 Forty winks
59 Govt. lending org.
62 Satanic
63 Vaudeville stars
65 Bottle part
66 Bestselling cookie
67 Put one over on
68 Change for a five
69 __ majesty (treason, e.g.)
70 Solemn appeals

DOWN

1 Cut down, as a tree
2 Theater award
3 Generic dog's name
4 Fuss
5 Do an electrical job
6 __ Le Pew
7 Regions
8 Public persona
9 L.A. team
10 '80s prime-time soap
11 Foreigner
12 Stretches across
13 Wrongful act, in law
18 Gives a dressing-down to
23 World leaders' meetings
25 Actress Farrow
26 Categorize
27 "If __ I Would Leave You"
28 Wharf
29 Any second now
33 Billiards stick
34 Open-handed blow
36 "Listen!"
37 Southernmost Great Lake
38 Disavow
41 Poem part
44 Make lace
48 Small handgun
50 Taken care of
51 Sanctuary
52 *Holiday* __ (skating show)
53 Sleeper's sound
54 Great expectations
56 Carson's successor
58 Bassoon relative
59 State of agitation
60 Johann Sebastian __
61 Poses a question
64 Coach Parseghian

68 BIG BUCKS

Richard Silvestri

ACROSS

1 Spaghetti, e.g.
6 Not us
10 College military grp.
14 The Ram
15 Angel topper
16 Poet Pound
17 Like a rich cobbler?
19 Frog kin
20 Rebel Turner
21 Put on a play
22 Fairy-tale opener
23 Like a rich paver?
26 Pertaining to stars
29 Infant
30 Back-to-health process, for short
31 Significant
34 Summery
37 Tabriz resident
38 Be in debt
39 Too big
41 Quayle or Rather
42 War horse
44 Clinic worker
45 High card
46 Brook
47 Like a rich farmer?
53 Piece of land
54 "Peachy!"
55 Slugger Gehrig
58 Afrikaner
59 Like a rich computer programmer?

62 "This __ outrage!"
63 British carbine
64 Recipient
65 London gallery
66 Bustle
67 Shell out

DOWN

1 Chess piece
2 Vicinity
3 Delta deposit
4 __ Aviv
5 Powdery residue
6 Greek letter
7 Chicago Bears founder
8 Pensive poem
9 California city
10 Verbal zinger
11 Atmospheric layer
12 Smidgen
13 Military student
18 Donkey: Ger.
23 Port of Algiers
24 Fig Newtons name
25 Home of the Blue Jays
26 Like the Negev
27 Vaccines
28 Comparative word
31 A Stooge
32 Wonderment
33 Clampett patriarch
34 At this point
35 Mountain in Thessaly

36 Abound
40 Small town
43 Wimbledon figure
45 Actor Brian
46 Oxford, for one
47 Custom
48 Word form for "twenty"
49 Terrific
50 Fifty past (the hour)
51 Couldn't stand
52 "Culture" word form
55 "I Walk the __" (Cash song)
56 Not decided
57 Secondhand
60 LP successors
61 Dance party

69 UTENSILS FOR YOUR PENCILS

Lee Weaver

ACROSS

1 Delhi dress
5 Like rich soil
10 Three-handed card game
14 Exuberance
15 City or circle preceder
16 Architect Saarinen
17 Male turkeys
18 Meat/vegetable mixtures
19 Lawyer: Abbr.
20 Annual football event
22 __ Park, CO
23 Winnie the Pooh's pal
24 Seed covering
25 Roman sea god
29 Napped leathers
31 Cease, to a sailor
32 Orderly
34 Dutch cheese
36 Brooch
37 Boise's state
38 Feel remorse
39 Reverberate
41 Garr or Hatcher
42 Knocks for a loop
44 Postponed indefinitely
46 West Indies islands
48 __-do-well
49 Bagel filling
50 Confuse
52 Hack novel
58 French Sudan, today
59 Photo tint
60 Inlet

61 Fruit drinks
62 Extraterrestrial
63 Not up yet
64 "Listen!"
65 Skeptical
66 Who's the __? (Danza sitcom)

DOWN

1 Matching groups
2 Baseball manager Felipe
3 Highway exit
4 Skirt panels
5 Capital of Portugal
6 Aware of
7 All over again
8 Kitten sound
9 Many mos.

10 By the shore
11 Large percussion instrument
12 Johnson of Laugh-In
13 Playthings
21 Disastrous defeat
22 Before, poetically
24 Family vehicle
25 Back of the neck
26 Push out
27 Alms seeker
28 Finished
29 Indian title
30 Spa offering
33 A sense organ
35 Army chow
37 Roman road

40 Slender, four-sided pillar
42 "Go away!"
43 City transportation
45 Loser at Gettysburg
47 New York city
50 Asian nursemaid
51 Baby word
52 Brazilian soccer great
53 Role for Ronny Howard
54 Wedding-cake feature
55 Timber wolf
56 Nights before
57 Cincinnati team
59 Gal of song

70 D DAY

Rich Norris

ACROSS

1 Metered vehicles
6 VCR outlets
9 Milk snake
14 Fight site
15 That guy
16 Concerto instrument
17 Computer component
19 Salad ingredient
20 Trump or Duck
22 Digital watch feature: Abbr.
23 Doohickeys
27 Fox hunter's cry
30 Workers' organizations
31 Sudden police action
32 __ way (not at all)
33 Team swimming game
38 Reading room
39 Wash-and-wear
41 Former Egypt-Syria alliance: Abbr.
42 Hates
44 Palindromic rock group
45 Smell bad
46 Wholesale unit
48 Benefactor, as of a college
51 Genuine
52 Mauna __
53 Poetic device
55 Peter of *Easy Rider*
58 Desert whirlwind
63 Ancient Peruvian
64 Sharp curve
65 Linda Lavin sitcom
66 Impoverished
67 Porker place
68 Cry of dismay

DOWN

1 Wee bit
2 Jackie's second
3 Signs, in a way
4 Sign
5 Make blue
6 Becomes sparser
7 __ *Las Vegas* (Presley film)
8 Process, as ore
9 Mil. address
10 Big racket
11 Exacta relative
12 Son of Cain
13 Mozart composition
18 Goes bad
21 Challenger
23 Tour leader
24 Building addition
25 Formal evening gathering
26 Icky stuff
28 NFL Hall-of-Famer Yale __
29 Backtalk
33 Keen perception
34 Imitate
35 Football scores: Abbr.
36 Cabinet department
37 Give an address
39 Made pictures
40 Garden tools
43 Corp. bigshot
44 As simple as __
46 Leave at the altar
47 Eventually
48 Mischievous
49 Nary a soul
50 Carnival attractions
51 Actress Spacek
54 Has to
56 June honoree
57 Some
59 Inventor Whitney
60 Celebrity, initially
61 Wintry hazard
62 Bandleader Brown

71 TIME FOR CHANGE

Norma Steinberg

ACROSS

1 Model Macpherson
5 Shoeman McAn
9 *The Trial* author Franz
14 Colorado ski town
15 Angelic corona
16 Prospero's servant
17 Bullets
18 Therefore
19 Monica of tennis
20 *Laverne & Shirley* star
23 Hair goos
24 Owns
25 Shoulder wrap
27 Play about Capote
29 Tachometer abbr.
32 Upper class
33 Minnesota Fats' game
34 Mets' stadium
35 Battle stations
38 Newspaper essay page
39 Boxing match
40 Writer Joyce Carol
41 Ave. crossers
42 Reverence
43 Batters' options
44 Donkey
46 Hourglass filling
47 Argue pettily
53 Devilfish
54 Arkin of *Chicago Hope*
55 Snack
57 Fancy tie
58 Ditka or Wallace

59 Way in
60 Divvy up
61 Congregational response
62 Stick around

DOWN

1 Zsa Zsa's sister
2 Reading light
3 Daiquiri ingredient
4 Stretched
5 "__ never believe me . . ."
6 Does damage to
7 Gymnast Korbut
8 Othello, e.g.
9 Buckwheat groats

10 Vicinities
11 Eat one's __ (have enough)
12 Boat part
13 Gore and D'Amato
21 More recent
22 Former Dolphins coach
25 Caught some z's
26 Dancer Gregory
27 Chef's hat
28 Drive out
29 Scarlett's Butler
30 Former Israeli PM
31 Church service
32 Personalities
33 Turn over earth

34 Sports-page listings
36 Demean
37 Circular
43 Outlaws
44 Cast member
45 Emulate Yamaguchi
46 Plumber's tool
47 Poet Ogden
48 Ancient Peruvian
49 Tibetan leader
50 Take __ view (disapprove)
51 Castle's protection
52 ¿*Cómo __ usted?*
53 Advanced degs.
56 "Yo!"

72 ALL AT SEA

Lee Weaver

ACROSS

1 Primary
6 Capp and Capone
9 Halloween disguises
14 Hawaiian "Hi!"
15 Positive vote
16 Be of use
17 More docile
18 Ordinance
19 Cowboy contest
20 Salon offering
23 Dessert choice
24 "Agnus __" (Mass movement)
25 GI show sponsor
28 Kuwaiti ruler
31 Tooth covering
36 Helps along temporarily
39 Author Calvino
40 Composer Stravinsky
41 Conceit
42 Change for a five
43 Tennis champ Evert
45 Falsify ore content
48 Agreement
50 Jump
51 Elevator compartment
52 Dawn goddess
54 Segments: Abbr.
56 Subject in a civics class
63 Wickerwork willow
64 Be obligated to
65 Buffet patron
68 Sierra __
69 On a pension: Abbr.
70 Patronize a rink
71 Fur-trading name
72 Many mos.
73 Ice pinnacle

DOWN

1 Dietary component
2 Dockworker's org.
3 Frolic boisterously
4 Part of the herd
5 Lingers awhile
6 Clan of the Cave Bear heroine
7 Tilt
8 Made logs
9 007's drink
10 State firmly
11 Actress Thompson
12 Ukraine capital
13 Blackthorn fruit
21 Interoffice note
22 Formerly named
25 New York city
26 Sounds of regret
27 Bakery enticements
29 Currier's partner
30 Fit for a queen
32 Powerful particle
33 Excessively enthusiastic
34 Actress Verdugo
35 Also-ran
37 Canal to Buffalo
38 Part in a play
44 One who scoffs
46 Finish-line feature
47 Suitability
49 Freight weight
53 Fairy tale, e.g.
55 Tent holder
56 Popular soft drink
57 Applications
58 Free-for-all
59 Clinton cabinet member
60 Wash-basin partner
61 Doggie doctors
62 Milky Way part
66 Greek H
67 VCR button

JUST DESSERTS

Lee Weaver

ACROSS

1 Scottish lake
5 Cast member
10 Western writer Grey
14 Taj Mahal site
15 Greene of *Bonanza*
16 "An apple __ . . ."
17 Bottomless
18 Pass into law
19 "Encore!"
20 Positive vote
21 Shoe-sole material
23 Encounters
25 Iroquoian Indians
26 Quaking trees
28 Singer Ross
30 Imperfection
31 Joins, as metal
32 Dine
35 Comments from Sandy
36 Small mountains
37 Maneuverable, as a yacht
38 British forces: Abbr.
39 Gyrates
40 Powerful beam
41 Bamboos, e.g.
42 Folkloric woodsman
43 Pay out
45 Winter coat
46 Simple task
49 Resort feature
52 Sea eagle
53 Give up the right to
54 Make a web
55 Min. fractions
56 Gunpowder ingredient
57 Punt, e.g.
58 Singles
59 Winter gliders
60 "Uh huh!"

DOWN

1 Titled woman
2 Pointed arch
3 Pristine used car
4 Prefix for hazard
5 Gives a warning
6 Highway markers
7 Fairway hazard
8 In the past
9 Born-again tires
10 South African country
11 Sun-dried brick
12 Nostrils
13 Ogler
21 Indian Head, e.g.
22 Coffee brewers
24 Wrigglers
26 At a distance
27 Poet Teasdale
28 Forest clearings
29 Troubles
31 Unmanageable
32 Extremely simple
33 Field of study
34 Sea swallow
36 Rural dances
37 Tug sharply
39 Russo of *Tin Cup*
40 Fishline adjunct
41 Niche
42 Bread makers
43 Fire-truck warning
44 Coventry cash
45 Worked on a road
46 Acapulco coin
47 Fall short
48 Refer to
50 12-point type
51 Egyptian cross
54 Shade of blue

74 TV REPAIRMEN

Rich Norris

ACROSS

1 Take __ (travel)
6 Not domesticated
11 FedEx rival
14 Doorbell sound
15 Like beer at a barbecue
16 Total
17 *M*A*S*H* doctor
19 Palindromic preposition
20 *Star Trek* helmsman
21 Universal ideal
22 Region
23 Teenage TV doctor
28 From the U.S.: Abbr.
30 Concert closer, often
31 Like some drives
33 Auctioneer's announcement
34 Rank below lt.
37 Small guns
39 Teaser
41 Paid announcements
42 Hawaiian necklaces
44 Marvelous
45 Iran, once
47 Pond denizens
48 '60s TV doctor
52 Kitchen emanation
53 Psyche parts
54 *On the __* (Kerouac book)
58 Bagel partner
59 '70s TV doctor
63 Numerical word form
64 For a specific purpose
65 Actress MacDowell
66 Go out with
67 Atmospheric layer
68 Take the helm

DOWN

1 Play parts
2 By way of, for short
3 Iranian monetary unit
4 Rude
5 __ talk (pregame ritual)
6 Search, as for food
7 Prohibits legally, as a strike
8 Hope-Crosby destination
9 Ludwig's lament
10 Actor Cariou
11 Computer operators
12 Tomato-sauce ingredient
13 Nasty campaign tactic
18 Ike's WWII command
22 Veneration
24 Baltimore team
25 Subj. for Keynes
26 Made, as a putt
27 Restaurant patron, at first
28 Litmus reddener
29 Unwieldy situation
31 Health resort
32 Paperwork processor
34 Blinds component
35 Precious stones
36 Attempt
38 Affirmative from Alberto
40 Respectfully submissive
43 __ Valley (high-tech region)
45 Each
46 Cite as evidence
48 Unwelcome surprises
49 Cherish
50 Guts
51 Biblical beast
55 Adjective for shoppe
56 Irish Rose's lover
57 Clothing factory employee
59 __ Tse-tung
60 Ax relative
61 Greek letter
62 Used to be

SOUND REASONING

Norma Steinberg

ACROSS

1 Diminishes
5 "__ want is a room somewhere . . ."
9 __-Magnon man
12 Appearance
13 Nary a soul
15 Levin and Gershwin
16 Ali's arena
18 Snack
19 Whichever
20 Automotive pioneer
21 Mistake–finder's shout
23 Channel marker
24 Part of the foot
25 Bricklayers
28 Sit-ins, e.g.
32 Choir section
33 Daily delivery
34 Fastener
35 Bridge coup
36 Judge's hammer
37 Pathway
38 Poi ingredient
39 Billfold stuffers
40 Burn slightly
41 Robin Hood's forest
43 Planted clues
44 Willy Loman's son
45 Fried-rice additive
46 Bush Chief of Staff
49 Identical
50 Winter bug
53 Singer Redding
54 45s
57 Desire
58 Fry lightly
59 Zilch
60 That girl
61 Very, in Versailles
62 Partridge's tree

DOWN

1 Napoleon home
2 Blessing
3 Square-shaped
4 Glide
5 Whites, to Chicanos
6 "Oh, my!"
7 Superman's girlfriend
8 Hostel
9 Gator's relative
10 Impetuous
11 DC workplace monitors
14 Chinese appetizer
15 Up the river
17 Parts of speech
22 Autumn mo.
23 Economic extremes
24 The Ram
25 Ship's poles
26 Koran subject
27 Rubberneck
28 Used macadam
29 Perspective
30 Slight coloration
31 Velocity
33 __ *La Mancha*
36 Mistakes
40 Ambulance sound
42 Take the gold
43 Neighborhood friends
45 Sticky stuff
46 Porcine females
47 Brigham Young's destination
48 WXY on a phone
49 Goad
50 Huge ice chunk
51 Actress Olin
52 Computer owner
55 Cereal grain
56 Macroeconomic indicator: Abbr.

76 HARD RAIN

Lee Weaver

ACROSS

1 Movie award
6 Islam holy city
11 Scale starts
14 Swiftly
15 Campfire remains
16 Wise bird
17 Fried cornmeal creations
19 African antelope
20 Not becoming
21 Shoe part
23 Gorilla or chimp
24 Pestle's partner
26 Surfaces of gems
30 Enjoy a favorite book
31 Mountains of Russia
32 Barbecue materials
33 Chromosome component
36 New Jersey NBA team
37 Macbeth's title
38 Ink spot
39 Perfume amount
40 Mountain top
41 Good: Sp.
42 Make happy
44 Soaking wet
45 Boy Scout units
46 James Bond, e.g.
47 Reasoning
48 Putting into office
53 Hole-punching gadget
54 At a diagonal
57 Afternoon social
58 Make happy
59 Nervous
60 Make a mistake
61 Blip producer
62 On the peevish side

DOWN

1 Honolulu's island
2 Whirled
3 Mama __ Elliot
4 Feel sore
5 Does over and over
6 Table wood
7 Catch sight of
8 Tai __ (martial art)
9 Average grade
10 Guarantees
11 Swam in a crouch
12 Deed holder
13 Speak unclearly
18 Refs' counterparts
22 Harper Valley grp.
24 Intended
25 Heraldic border
26 Rainy-day money, e.g.
27 Vicinity
28 Second-story man
29 Overhead trains
30 Friars event
32 Gourmet cooks
34 Not any
35 Like __ of bricks
37 Fall over one's feet
38 Baby bloomer
40 Track official
41 Protest tactic
43 Luau dip
44 Building detail, for short
45 Babel structure
46 More cunning
47 Running behind
48 Sundance's girlfriend
49 Genealogy chart
50 B&Bs
51 Bird's shelter
52 Actor Joel
55 Dockworker's org.
56 Small amount

77 TAKING UP SPACE

Mary Brindamour

ACROSS

1 Actor Ladd
5 Short swims
9 Walks back and forth
14 Actress Kedrova
15 Buffalo's lake
16 Residence
17 Stargazer's device
19 Too thin
20 Mature
21 Worked with rattan
22 Lab heaters
23 Like some cars
25 Wooden shoe
27 Lend __ (listen)
30 Twilled
33 Dad's brother
36 Scrumptious
38 __-Locka, FL
39 Chime
40 Takes to the pawnshop
41 Was obligated to
42 Aykroyd or Rather
43 __ Island (Big Apple amusement area)
44 Old Norse poems
45 Sage
47 Ancient lute
49 Annuls
51 Not these
55 McQueen of movies
57 Metrical feet
60 Grassy meadow
61 Actress Sophia
62 Astronaut's outfit
64 Disassociated
65 Largest continent
66 Advantage
67 Thaws
68 Fasting time
69 Make one's way

DOWN

1 Mass site
2 Feudal superior
3 *Manhattan* director
4 Aberdeen denial
5 Century component
6 Do a laundry job
7 Plumbing part
8 Garden starters
9 Hair style
10 Nuisance stopper
11 Lift-off preceder
12 Writer Ferber
13 TVs
18 Seascape, for one
24 Like redwoods
26 Performances
28 "This must weigh __!"
29 Indy participant
31 Fencer's sword
32 Most Little League coaches
33 Formal hair style
34 At hand
35 Cape in Florida
37 A terrier
40 Weeded
41 "That hurts!"
43 Law firm's customers
44 Make a new bow
46 Surreptitious
48 Lynx
50 Cordage fiber
52 Circumvent
53 Hold sway
54 Stuffed
55 Shut with a bang
56 Drink to excess
58 Church area
59 Popular street name
63 Stitch

78 TIGHT SPOTS

Rich Norris

ACROSS
1 Caged chirper
7 Calamine target
11 Arafat's org.
14 *Seinfeld* character
15 Scored 100
16 Thompson of *Caroline in the City*
17 Logical propositions
18 Piece of cake, so to speak
20 Very, in Vichy
21 Scout's doing
22 911 responders: Abbr.
23 Toast topping
27 "__ There Eyes"
28 Consumer
30 Mil. fliers' hangout
33 Son of Cain
36 Yankees shortstop Derek
38 Grinning from ear __
40 Ode title opening
41 Paragon
42 Carpentry, e.g.
43 Long-plumed heron
45 ADA member
46 Double Windsor, e.g.
47 Helper: Abbr.
49 Cost increase consequence
56 Brake pad
58 Nephew of Abel
59 Not very busy
60 Sprain treatment
62 Well-pitched
64 Chemical ending
65 Englishman's exclamation
66 Bird attraction
67 CPA's concern
68 __ time (never)
69 Bridge builder's concern

DOWN
1 Boston cagers, for short
2 On one's toes
3 Stool pigeon, e.g.
4 Has in one's sights
5 Genetic info transmitter
6 "Of course!"
7 Bread pro
8 Less receptive
9 Tot's sleep aid?
10 Ames and Wynn
11 Went down dramatically
12 Went away
13 Boors
19 Made fun of
21 Reassign, in a way
24 Cabbie's question
25 Actor Kingsley
26 Karate relative
29 Peruse
30 Lwyr.
31 Road junction
32 Lanky ones
34 Tooth
35 Bother persistently
37 Literary monogram
39 Cherished
44 Title of respect: Abbr.
48 Examiner
50 Magnificent meal
51 Quechua speaker
52 Ginza locale
53 Get away from
54 Sectors
55 Spouted vessels
56 Strikebreaker
57 Toot one's own horn
61 Actress Zadora
62 Conditions
63 Court divider

80 IT'S ABOUT TIME!

Rich Norris

ACROSS

1 Avoid an F
5 Examine closely
9 Rigatoni, for one
14 General vicinity
15 Lotto relative
16 Freeway fillers
17 *The Time Machine* actor
19 Tread heavily
20 "__ little teapot . . ."
21 Happy-hour order
22 Consumer concerns
23 *A Time to Kill* actress
27 Burgle
28 Handle carelessly
29 Dispensable candy
32 Bird's claw
35 Barbecue accessories
36 Mont. neighbor
37 "Time __, pencils down"
38 Timely words
39 Comedian Wilson
40 Put the kibosh on
41 *Roots* author
42 Losing propositions?
43 Fraternity letter
44 *Der __* (Adenauer)
45 Assistance
46 "Time Is on My Side" group
52 Swallowlike birds
54 Tiebreakers: Abbr.
55 __ Miss
56 More than annoyed
57 *Time* founder

60 In time
61 Creme-filled cookie
62 "It's __ to Tell a Lie"
63 Admits customers
64 Scorecard numbers
65 "Love __" (Beatles song)

DOWN

1 Helen's abductor
2 Scent
3 Family car
4 Took a load off
5 '70s space station
6 Autograph hound's target
7 Pitch __-hitter
8 Postal Creed word
9 Checks the grounds
10 Goldfinger's first name
11 Accumulate
12 Big book
13 Egyptian cobras
18 Moses' brother
22 Mickey's mutt
24 Egg __ soup
25 A whole bunch
26 Congregation
30 Revise copy
31 Uses a ray gun
32 Coloring
33 China's continent
34 Enjoy oneself to the hilt

35 Conductor Sir Georg
38 Shopping meccas
39 Supposed common dog name
41 Summer tops
42 Scatterbrained
45 Houston nine
47 Many times
48 His time has run out
49 Of __ (unavailing)
50 Spanish hero
51 "__ evil, hear . . ."
52 Farm building
53 Prepare a gift
57 School dance
58 Time period
59 Hasty escape

79 FRANKLY SPEAKING

Norma Steinberg

ACROSS

1 Boo-boo
5 Oranges' coverings
10 Piece of information
14 Make bye-bye
15 Longbow ammo
16 "Now __ me down to sleep . . ."
17 Trendsetting
19 Thpeak like thith
20 Brooch
21 Used to be
22 Newspaper name
24 Add salt to, e.g.
26 '96 presidential candidate
27 Put __ (store)
29 Gloomy
33 Balkan native
36 Average
38 Home of the Dolphins
39 King of the road
40 Map close-up
42 Chuck-wagon food
43 ". . . __ by land . . ."
45 Roman garb
46 Famous loch
47 London driver's purchase
49 Word form for "sleep"
51 Liberates
53 Head man
57 Pilot

60 Innovative: Ger.
61 Chafe
62 Tubular pasta
63 Mark Twain, e.g.
66 Consumer
67 Perfect
68 Wedding vows
69 Like a poor excuse
70 Office furniture
71 Pierre's dad

DOWN

1 Trades
2 "C'est __!"
3 An ex–Mrs. Trump
4 Pigsty
5 Composer for the violin
6 Historical periods
7 Act humanly?
8 Vacation home
9 Attests
10 Expensive steak
11 Dismounted
12 Acting group
13 Use a keyboard
18 Groupings on the ark
23 Kind of lens
25 Social ease
26 Individuals
28 "__ make me laugh!"
30 Unadorned
31 Big birds
32 Barbecue servings
33 Go to the mall
34 Solo
35 Lend a hand, perhaps
37 Prefix for bucks
41 North Carolinians
44 Stronghold
48 Brezhnev of Russia
50 Brilliant move
52 Eat away at
54 Unrefined
55 Drollery
56 Too big
57 Blue, in Baja
58 Passport stamp
59 Line-__ veto
60 Mont. neighbor
64 "Bonjour, __ amis!"
65 Backtalk

81 FORE-SIGHT

Lee Weaver

ACROSS

1 Spider's creations
5 __ McNally
9 Birthday bash
14 All over again
15 Eternally
16 Entertain
17 Outfit for Nero
18 Mrs. Dithers
19 Reb's foes
20 Triple-decker lunch
23 Gretel's companion
24 Org. for hunters
25 Except
28 Hoofbeat sound
31 Landed property
33 Hurry off
37 Casual tops
39 Designer Chanel
40 Impose a levy
41 Run into
42 Financially behind
45 Towel again
46 Black Sea port
47 Neutral color
49 "__ on your life!"
50 Spy org.
52 Houston team
57 Assume responsibility
60 Inexpensive
63 Golda of Israel
64 *The King* __
65 "If You Knew __ . . ."
66 European volcano
67 Bridle part
68 Current style
69 Saucer
70 Hunt for

DOWN

1 Keep an eye on
2 __ *Gay*
3 Already started
4 Mops the deck
5 Bring to mind
6 Shakespeare's river
7 Social misfit
8 Sketched
9 Eschew charge cards
10 Asian nursemaid
11 Seek office
12 Admonisher's sound
13 Thumbs-up vote
21 Religious offshoot
22 Really riles
25 Revealed
26 Complete
27 On the peevish side
29 Director Preminger
30 Author Norman Vincent
32 *Newsweek* rival
33 Offspring
34 Townhouse type
35 Group of eight
36 Sounds of awe
38 CEO, e.g.
43 Flew the coop
44 Head covering
45 Artful dodge
48 Stadium cheers
51 Equipped for battle
53 Skiers' conveyances
54 Indian queen
55 Song from the past
56 Move furtively
57 Eve's oldest
58 Bigfoot cousin
59 Pie pans
60 St. Louis clock setting
61 *Ben-*__
62 U-turn from WNW

82 NEUTRAL CORNERS

Norma Steinberg

ACROSS

1 Ear part
5 Cincinnati team
9 Tick off
13 Pinnacle
14 Memo words
15 Chris of tennis
17 Spouse
18 Spanish custard
19 Unbroken
20 Keep from employment
22 French city
23 Nuthatch's home
24 Bottomless pit
25 Wise person
28 Morsel
30 Officiated at tea
32 Dove call
33 Newspaper page
37 Where to find Turkey
39 Away from the center
41 Theater presentation
42 Part of a circle
44 Group's possessive
45 Stevenson of *M*A*S*H*
48 Vases
49 Young horses
51 Weaving machine
53 Bully
54 Memorable abolitionist
59 Plains formation
60 Author Leon
61 Modeling material

62 Good news for anglers
63 Small insect
64 Unimportant
65 Ripped
66 Annoying one
67 Soldier's place

DOWN

1 Meek one
2 Milky gem
3 Greek letter
4 Pres. or Treas.
5 Hunting weapon
6 Sign up
7 Immoderate
8 Mailed
9 Iron-rich mountain range
10 Self-imposed isolation
11 Cuts down
12 Side order
16 Gridiron scores: Abbr.
21 Leg parts
24 Circa
25 Music genre
26 Halo
27 Intelligence
29 "Inka Dinka __"
30 Vitality
31 TV controls
34 "No __, no gain"
35 Goofs
36 Dental degree: Abbr.
38 "We __ not amused!"
40 Hitchhiker's digit

43 Dieter's measurement
46 *Fawlty Towers* star
47 Part of a perfect-game description
49 Product
50 __ LUNCH (store sign)
52 Beginning
53 Consumer advisory agcy.
54 Checkers move
55 Canadian cops: Abbr.
56 Butter alternative
57 Armed conflicts
58 Sergei's negative

83 IN THE BALLPARK

Norma Steinberg

ACROSS
1 Sharp taste
5 Severe
10 Bedouin
14 Skin-cream ingredient
15 Carroll heroine
16 Actress Miles
17 No threat
19 Lazily
20 Dumbfound
21 Part of a fork
22 Bible book
23 Desperately
25 Aspiration
27 Actor O'Neal
29 Skeptical one
32 Waller of jazz
35 Newspaperman Greeley
39 Baseball bat wood
40 Lyricist Gershwin
41 Like a pioneer's wagon
42 Actor Gulager
43 Gender
44 Did nothing
45 Consider
46 Was obligated
48 Ump's call
50 Commands
54 Far away
58 *M*A*S*H* star
60 Comic Carvey
62 Nincompoops
63 Omen, e.g.
64 Distances in a kids' game
66 With: Fr.
67 Dramatic whisper
68 Cleveland's lake
69 Pierre's pop
70 Chill out
71 Fathers

DOWN
1 South American appetizers
2 Memorable mission
3 Type of bond
4 Coots
5 Bowler or beret
6 Got down
7 Uncompromising
8 Commotion
9 "__ Johnny!"
10 Bird house
11 '50s scare
12 Woody Guthrie's kid
13 Howls at the moon
18 Depend
24 Boor
26 Frosted
28 __ Scotia
30 Wight, for one
31 Pal
32 Salmon or shad
33 Neighborhood
34 IRS quarry
36 Gridiron arbiter
37 God of war
38 Fragrant wood
41 Lump of earth
45 Took down a peg
47 Hypnotic state
49 Govt. agents
51 __ Allan Poe
52 Salary increase
53 Slow-moving animal
55 *Norma* or *Carmen*
56 Lukewarm
57 Curvy letters
58 Letters on a memo
59 Exist
61 Cost an arm __ leg
65 John Ritter's father

84 UNREAL ATTORNEYS

Rich Norris

ACROSS

1 Locking device
5 Very fast
10 Flower part
14 Concept
15 Love, in Livorno
16 Singing sound
17 Raymond Burr role
19 Mom's sister
20 Confused situation
21 Eastern discipline
22 Debate
23 Entr'__
25 Hothouse plant
26 Gregory Peck role
31 Plaid pattern
32 Birds: Lat.
33 Corp. alias
36 Radio guy Don
37 Wide valleys
39 Drescher of *The Nanny*
40 Golf prop
41 Very, in Vichy
42 Ohio city
44 Susan Dey role
46 Earthy colours
49 Prefix for while
50 Incite, as havoc
51 Christmas tree
53 Down source
57 Terra firma
58 Andy Griffith role
60 Feminine ending
61 Invite to enter
62 Plumb crazy
63 Herbal quaffs
64 Composer Jule
65 Iowa city

DOWN

1 Rose parts
2 Arabian Sea gulf
3 Blood fluids
4 Ice-cream desserts
5 Ewe's mate
6 Astonishes
7 Sit for a photo
8 Fe
9 Reading room
10 Laundry stiffener
11 Leathery
12 Boredom
13 Apportioned
18 New Mexico state flower
22 Circle parts
24 Frozen wastelands
25 Brigadier general's designation
26 Working hard
27 Bring under control
28 With 29 Down, type of test
29 See 28 Down
30 "__ Gotta Be Me"
33 Comic Carey
34 Said, as "farewell"
35 Soon
38 NRC predecessor
39 Small naval unit
41 Arduous journey
43 Beginning
44 Evaluates
45 Exterminator's concern
46 Nocturnal youngster
47 Construction-site sight
48 Salon color
51 Slug or song ending
52 Black
54 Adverse fate
55 Behold, to Brutus
56 Bygone theatres
58 Coll. degrees
59 Chemical ending

85 ON BOARDS

Bob Lubbers

ACROSS

1 Give off
5 Swimmer Buster
11 Animation unit
14 Teri of *Tootsie*
15 Greetings
16 High card
17 Dinner-table speck
19 A Bobbsey twin
20 Power-broker initials
21 Cruise-ship attendant
23 Buddy of *Barnaby Jones*
26 Mouse menacer
28 Comic Johnson
29 Choral pieces
31 Metal joiner
33 "Made in the __"
34 Alternatively
36 Faction
41 Oregon city
42 Actress Charlotte
44 Lined diagrams
47 Transmit, as from NBC
50 Morays
51 Blockhead
52 Sicily neighbor
53 Swears (to)
56 Smack
57 Edge
58 One way to tie a tie
64 *Bambi* aunt
65 Sports halls
66 "Dies __"
67 Actor Duryea
68 Scold
69 Archibald of the NBA

DOWN

1 Omelet need
2 Scratch
3 Lyricist Gershwin
4 Hot-plate holder
5 Use a hatchet
6 Sports judge
7 Capp and Pacino
8 Blowout
9 Metal fastener
10 Princely Italian family
11 Vile rumor
12 Card game
13 Borrower's opposite
18 Actress Foch
22 Hidden kid in picture books
23 French coin
24 Striped fish
25 Piece of cake
26 Poem division
27 Declares
30 Color shades
31 George of *Just Shoot Me*
32 Boat propeller
35 Attempts
37 Discontinuance
38 Suffix of approximation
39 Russian river
40 Done with
43 Greek vowel
44 __ up (got ready)
45 Eye part
46 *Nashville* director
48 Abu Dhabi chief
49 Marsh plant
51 Actor Ed
54 Mop
55 Grow weary
56 Waterer's need
59 Genetic stuff
60 Made a lap
61 New Deal org.
62 Cereal grain
63 Golf prop

86 FAMILY FILMS

Randy Sowell

ACROSS

1 Hillary, to Bill
5 Grain to be ground
10 Clenched hand
14 Farm tools
15 Come back to mind
16 Hammett hound
17 Roz Russell film of '58
19 Sports group
20 Submissions to eds.
21 Bit attachment
22 Area of influence
24 Transmitted
25 German admiral of WWI
26 Splotches
29 Title for Mao
33 Time interval
34 Membership money
35 Vanished
36 Like crazy
37 "__ Johnny!"
38 Probability quote
39 Went quickly
40 Evict
41 Woo
42 Ingress
44 Little ladies
45 Leg joint
46 Paella ingredient
47 Security
50 Physicist Ernst
51 The Buckeyes' sch.

54 __ impasse (stuck)
55 Reagan film of '38
58 "__ Free"
59 Spine-tingling
60 Big name in locks
61 Tube trophy
62 John of rock
63 BPOE members

DOWN

1 Sound of impact
2 Debtors' notes
3 Swampy areas
4 NH clock setting
5 Salad material
6 Send payment
7 "__ do anything better than you"
8 Total
9 Enter unlawfully
10 Cary Grant film of '64
11 Oracle's words
12 Night sky sight
13 Hardly exciting
18 Actress Dunne
23 JFK Library architect
24 Roz Russell film of '46
25 Halloween garb
26 Blackboard
27 Falcon's toenail
28 Left, at sea
29 Gypsy's revenge

30 __ operandi
31 Conductor Previn
32 Avian abodes
34 Tennis tie
37 Busy buzzer
41 Hidden supply
43 *Them!* critter
44 Forest growth
46 Numerical relation
47 Kemo __
48 Energy source
49 Old MacDonald had one
50 Humorist Sahl
51 Spoken
52 Polio fighter
53 Some Sioux
56 Fam. member
57 Bread grain

87 LADIES DAY

Bob Lubbers

ACROSS

1 Newborn
5 Thunder god
9 Bacall's mate
14 Bide-__ Home
15 Nevada city
16 British nobles
17 Actress Perlman
18 Vicinity
19 Leaning
20 Diagonally
23 Ready
24 City of canals
27 Golf gadget
28 Farrow or Sara
30 Sense of tone
31 Fishing pole
32 Mr. Brezhnev
34 "Uh-oh!"
35 Early yarn machine
39 *Grapes of Wrath* name
40 Prepares broccoli, perhaps
41 Scull seat
42 Before, to a poet
44 Troy, N.Y. campus
45 Boxing victories, for short
48 Actor Lorne
50 Mountainous, in a way
52 Timid one
56 Overture, for short
58 ". . . with a banjo on my __"

59 Energy source
60 Follow behind
61 Summer coolers
62 Camper's need
63 Fibs
64 Olden days
65 Approximately

DOWN

1 Hound, as a dog
2 Once in __ (sometimes)
3 Scarab
4 Irish poet
5 Tire grip
6 Good-deed doer
7 Unique thing
8 Chestnut horse

9 All-purpose check payee
10 Of a grain
11 Football field
12 Ailing
13 Superlative suffix
21 Saudi Arabia neighbor
22 Gabor or Perón
25 Duplicate
26 Asner and Wynn
29 Flavorful herb
30 Lawn tool
32 Cap
33 Bank acct. yield
34 Switch positions
35 Fly high

36 Part of PG
37 Made in Tokyo
38 Writer Zola
39 Trot
42 Signs up
43 Minister: Abbr.
45 Out of __ (awry)
46 Steak topping
47 "Things aren't what they __ be"
49 Spooky
51 Greek philosopher
53 Approve
54 Take apart
55 Fortune-teller
56 Addams Family cousin
57 Gun owners' org.

Bob Frank

ACROSS

1. Danson and Koppel
5. File
9. Female honorific
14. Concept
15. Singer Fitzgerald
16. Linda Lavin role
17. Carillon item
18. "Can we talk?" comedienne
20. Part of ILGWU
21. Electrical resistance unit
22. Gladdens
23. Ancient Mideast kingdom
25. Consumed
26. Sports spectator
27. Lens opening
32. Aladdin's helper
35. Like Mozart's music
36. Tony Award relative
37. Collared garment
38. In the dumps
39. Type of pen
41. Closes tightly
42. Not to be consumed
43. Mid.
44. Wriggling fish
45. Bureau sections
49. More limber
53. Opponent
54. Nabisco bestseller
55. *Jury Duty* star
57. Pitcher Hershiser
58. Sandy's owner
59. Tap trouble
60. Medicinal measure
61. Position
62. Meadows
63. Winter vehicle

DOWN

1. Shin bone
2. Barbara and Anthony
3. Shoulder muscles, for short
4. *The Flying Nun* star
5. Unite once again
6. Hawaiian greeting
7. Close abruptly
8. God of woods
9. Padded envelopes
10. Edison's middle name
11. Japanese legislature
12. Land measure
13. Military cafeteria
19. Give a make-up exam
24. __ Dawn Chong
25. Separated
27. Dress style
28. '97 Masters winner
29. USC rival
30. Actor Julia
31. *Desire Under the __*
32. Asian desert
33. Abba of Israel
34. White or Blue river
35. Put on ice
37. Gets serious
40. In one's cups
41. RR depot
43. Obnoxious ones
45. *Andrea __* (ill-fated ship)
46. Swashbuckler Flynn
47. Della or Pee Wee
48. Did a shoe repair
49. Health resorts
50. Huff
51. Mystical symbol
52. Pelvic bones
53. Warning on the links
56. "Good" cholesterol: Abbr.

89 INSTRUMENTAL

Bob Lubbers

ACROSS

1 Brother of Cain
5 Charley horse
9 Buddies
13 Gaucho's device
14 Winter forecast
16 EPA subject
17 "Son of __ !"
18 __ firma
19 Disavow
20 Dabble
23 Golf peg
24 Sea eagle
25 Gladden
29 *Steppenwolf* author
31 Trial balloon
32 Fur magnate
35 Treater's words
37 Word form for "three"
38 Brag
42 Forty winks
43 Like __ of bricks
44 Calms
45 More satanic
48 Yearns (for)
50 Scout's job, for short
51 Menlo Park initials
52 __ carte
55 Feel optimistic
60 Poet Teasdale
63 Singly
64 Low in fat
65 All tied up
66 Ore digger
67 Rescue
68 Rolls of bills
69 Striped fish
70 Part of USA

DOWN

1 Sternward
2 *Maltese Falcon* star's nickname
3 Avoid capture
4 Alight
5 Fall flowers
6 Empties
7 Mister: Ger.
8 Architect Saarinen
9 Sell from a pushcart
10 Expert
11 Actor Chaney
12 Foxy
15 Greek letter
21 Dubious
22 Born: Fr.
26 Female voices
27 Pied-à-__ (second home)
28 Gray and Moran
29 In which way
30 Sign up
31 Not many
32 Daisy Mae's mate
33 Toil
34 Subject
36 Unmodulated voices
39 Boat propeller
40 Mideast desert
41 Owns
46 Ella and Joshua
47 Wind direction: Abbr.
49 Ombudsman Ralph's kin
52 Nautical direction
53 Exit
54 *Roots* Emmy-winner Ed
56 Scottish cap
57 Smooth-talking
58 O'Neill's daughter
59 *Casablanca* heroine
60 Stitch
61 Actress Gardner
62 Cerise or cherry

90 TWO FIRSTS

Norma Steinberg

ACROSS

1 Little wave
7 Undivided
10 "Yuck!"
13 Unscrupulous
14 Income
16 *Seinfeld* actor
18 Mellowed
19 Bad word in pinball
20 John __ Passos
21 "For __ a jolly good fellow"
22 Sty
23 Gridiron scores: Abbr.
25 Hot tub
28 Beethoven opera
30 Ugly Duckling's parent
31 "__ Old Cowhand"
33 Flightless bird
34 Small horse
35 *Babes in Toyland* composer
39 Tirade
40 Chamomile brew
41 Some deer
42 Env. stuffings
43 North Carolinian
46 Actress West
47 Leader of the Seven Dwarfs
48 Height: Abbr.
49 IRS employee
52 Russian space station
54 Infield covering
56 Soon
57 Revolutionary War turncoat

60 Canned fish
61 Come to terms
62 Broke a fast
63 British sports cars
64 Prey on one's mind

DOWN

1 Indian ruler
2 Mental picture
3 Affectations
4 Nudge
5 Office-wide computer hookup: Abbr.
6 Walking on air
7 Russian city
8 Subsequently
9 Zsa Zsa's sister
10 Disassemble
11 Unconfident estimation
12 That girl
15 Comes to a finale
17 Out of __ (unruly)
22 Half a quart
24 Gloomy
26 Trousers
27 Some
28 Data
29 Composer of *The Merry Widow*
30 Interval
31 Marla's predecessor
32 Thanksgiving pie choice
36 Director Preminger

37 Combining chemically
38 Borscht ingredient
39 Sleep phenom.
44 Playwright Moss
45 City on the Rio Grande
47 __ Scott Decision
49 $100
50 Trend-measuring questions
51 South American peaks
53 About
55 Superior serves
56 Tiny farm animals
57 Explorers' grp.
58 Poorly lit
59 Civil War soldier

91 HOW MANY?

Bob Lubbers

ACROSS

1 Waterproof covering
5 Dissention
11 Dentist's deg.
14 Needle case
15 Suit maker
16 Congressman: Abbr.
17 Just in time
19 "__ pig's eye!"
20 '90s music style
21 Attempt
23 Festoon
26 Bikini top
27 Dole (out)
28 Salad-dressing ingredient
30 Dress styles
32 Picnic pest
33 Bernadette's shrine
36 Monroe/Lemmon film of '59
41 Kansas city
42 __ la la
44 "This __ Love"
47 Bellies
50 Hebrew month
51 Overhead railroads
53 Allays
54 Florida Indian
57 Craze
58 "Be Prepared" grp.
59 "Ring-around-the-rosey" ending
64 Lwyr.
65 Nebraska river
66 Pennsylvania port
67 Laugh syllable
68 Talked back
69 Actress Russo

DOWN

1 Midmorning
2 From __ Z
3 Accept the nomination
4 Designer Cardin
5 "Halt!"
6 The way, to Lao-tzu
7 Stair part
8 Actress Massey
9 Nourishment
10 Seabird
11 Highly motivated
12 Designate
13 Extra parts
18 Sharp flavor
22 Pennsylvania sect
23 Actress Gardner
24 Rackets
25 Aware of
26 One way to cook
29 Kate's TV pal
30 Arles farewell
31 Allow
34 Don Ho's instrument
35 Apartment fees
37 Word form for "mother"
38 Recede
39 Elevator inventor
40 Corner, in a way
43 Dunderhead
44 Algiers district
45 "__ Fideles"
46 Quarterback Joe
48 Repast
49 More peeved
51 Raines and Fitzgerald
52 Ring jabs
55 Dozes
56 __ podrida
57 Took off
60 Consumed
61 Mine load
62 Come in first
63 Society-page word

92 RURAL ROLES

Patrick Jordan

ACROSS

1 Aspiration
5 He stares at stars
10 Halloween costume part
14 Plowing pair
15 Venture a viewpoint
16 Tangelo variety
17 Object to
18 Snake poison
19 Ring out
20 Summer hrs. in St. Pete
21 *Beverly Hillbillies* role
23 Farm machine
25 Fish eggs
26 '40s rural film couple
33 Severe
35 Colosseum site
36 Demonstrate
37 Boater or bowler
38 Imitated a crow
39 Find a purpose for
40 High cards in poker
42 Ready for business
43 Seeks
45 Edgar Bergen dummy
48 WSW opposite
49 Actor Borgnine
52 Old-time radio rural pair
58 Cheer from the bleachers
59 Evangelist Roberts
60 "__ you loud and clear!"
61 Swedish rock group
62 Stare at
63 Type of marble
64 Disney or Whitman
65 Jury member
66 Eminent
67 Looks at

DOWN

1 Greek epic poet
2 Nitrous __
3 Poetic rhythm pattern
4 Gridiron position
5 Oversee the state
6 Imitated
7 Galvanizing element
8 Organic compound
9 Made a comment
10 Jim Henson had a hand in them
11 *A Death in the Family* novelist
12 Thin plank
13 Scot's garb
21 Billie __ King
22 Scowling
24 Golfer's standard
27 Curtain
28 Energy
29 Congregation's affirmations
30 Ontario city
31 Disoriented
32 Meadow mamas
33 Counterfeit
34 Folded fast food
38 A stand-up guy?
41 Thief
43 Mister, in Munich
44 Coffee vessel
46 Bed-and-breakfast
47 Was obliged (to)
50 Weasel relative
51 "__ all, folks!"
52 Bowknot feature
53 Strong motivation
54 Drake or tom
55 Jason's ship
56 Rhythm
57 NBA Hall-of-Famer Archibald
61 Reverence

93

WATER LOG

Bob Lubbers

ACROSS

1 Fuel type
4 Master, on safari
9 "__ la vista"
14 Building site
15 Consumed
16 Come in
17 Boston Bruin legend
18 Ride the remote
20 Pile
22 The Emerald Isle
23 Seamen
26 Author Hemingway
30 Listen up
32 Western bar
34 Costa del __
36 Achy spots
38 Tribute
39 __ Called Horse
41 Flower part
43 Go berserk
44 Shoe string
45 Brazilian seaport
47 Change color
48 Topics
51 Enticers
53 Handsome young man
55 Tropical fruits
58 Pub drinks
60 Photographer Adams
61 Door trim
67 Word form for "three"
68 Worship
69 "Mule Train" singer Frankie
70 German article
71 Stairway post
72 Heavens above
73 Actress Ryan

DOWN

1 Shiny finish
2 Blood line
3 Strict
4 Summons
5 Baby's cry
6 One __ time
7 Hawaiian state bird
8 Warbucks' ward
9 Montana's capital
10 Response to a ques.
11 Alphabetic trio
12 Colonizer's holding: Abbr.
13 Barking sound
19 Drops the ball
21 Actor Gulager
24 Classic cars
25 Fire alarm
27 Moose relatives
28 Stereo, e.g.
29 NBC morning show
31 Himalayan kingdom
33 Yup's opposite
34 Popcorn seasoning
35 Nebraska Indian
37 Took notice
40 Verne captain
42 Zhivago's love
46 School glue name
49 Nail polish
50 Missile housing
52 Took off
54 Peddles
56 Condor's nest
57 David's weapon
59 Minn. neighbor
61 Is able to
62 Poetic form
63 Promise
64 Before, to the Bard
65 Square root of IX
66 Wind dir.

94 GRID PLAY

Rich Norris

ACROSS

1 Relative by marriage
6 Mortal
11 Like FDR's Deal
14 Put up with
15 Clear the board
16 Eggs
17 Flirted with
19 Nonsense
20 Gold measure
21 Toll road, for short
22 Most insinuating
26 Privilege loser, often
28 Make available for sale
31 Red-wrapped cheeses
32 Evans' partner
33 Food shop
34 Singer Tucker
36 Oklahoma city
40 Indira Gandhi's father
42 Hackneyed
43 Really enjoyed
46 Stevenson of *M*A*S*H*
48 Investigates anew, as a case
49 Woeful word
50 "___ Get Started With You"
52 Recyclable item
53 Forced to retreat
59 Circle part
60 Tim or Steve
61 Ruling class
62 Tiny
63 Untended, as a lawn
64 Like some stadiums

DOWN

1 "___ Woman" (Reddy tune)
2 Hoopsters' org.
3 Cover
4 Fruity drink
5 Enervates
6 Fireside setting
7 Sky bear
8 Schooner feature
9 Simile divider
10 Court divider
11 Retailer's guarantee
12 Draw forth
13 Tend the shrubs
18 Gone by
21 Prepare for a kiss
22 Zoomed
23 Art studio subject
24 Type *like this*: Abbr.
25 Chain reaction pieces
26 Edison's middle name
27 ___ constrictor
29 Boredom
30 Lad
34 "Easier said ___ done"
35 Covenant holder
37 Nick at ___
38 "Blame ___ the Bossa Nova"
39 Dict. entries
41 JFK posting
42 Having protrusions, as gears
43 Quick look
44 Nook partner
45 English county
46 Large parrot
47 ___ Boothe Luce
50 Do nothing
51 Dorm resident
53 Speak hesitantly
54 Pub pint
55 "Hold On Tight" band
56 Edge
57 Westen Indian
58 Actor Beatty

95 THE BUCKET

Lee Weaver

ACROSS
1 Story
5 Ice-cream utensil
10 German river
14 Felt sorry about
15 Telephone greeting
16 Roman emperor
17 Jason's ship
18 Good-for-nothing
19 Actress Stapleton
20 Atlas item
21 Low walls used as a defense in battle
23 Employers
25 Salary increase
26 Eagle's claws
28 Country gallant
30 Distribute
31 Emerald, essentially
32 Madison's state: Abbr.
35 Weight-loss program
36 Round roofs
37 Julep enhancer
38 Sun. talk
39 First Soviet premier
40 Prom, e.g.
41 Shoe ties
42 Looked for
43 Raccoon's cousin
45 Student of Zeno
46 Suzanne Somers' exercise gadget
49 Very popular
52 New Haven campus
53 In the know
54 Christmas visitors
55 Wharf
56 Exhibited fondness
57 Per __ (daily)
58 Comes to a halt
59 Lots and lots
60 Genealogy chart

DOWN
1 Trolley relative
2 Mystical emanation
3 Practical joker
4 Tokyo, once
5 Prepares eggs by baking
6 Gives up, as territory
7 Pedro's pot
8 Spanish cheers
9 Plays the part of
10 Enforce with authority
11 Sly looks
12 Sedan slower
13 Ages upon ages
21 Proclivity
22 Bemoan
24 Flue fallout
26 Tiny amounts
27 "I cannot tell __"
28 Road rigs
29 Small songbird
31 Fido's reward
32 Fireside seating
33 Part of a foot
34 Undo a dele
36 Topic in arithmetic
37 Hawaiian island
39 Thin slat
40 Entryway
41 Dark brews
42 War horses
43 __-link fence
44 Ended the squeak
45 Scatter (about)
46 Use a keyboard
47 MP's quarry
48 Rescue
50 Curved molding
51 *Newsweek* competitor
54 Summer hrs. in Denver

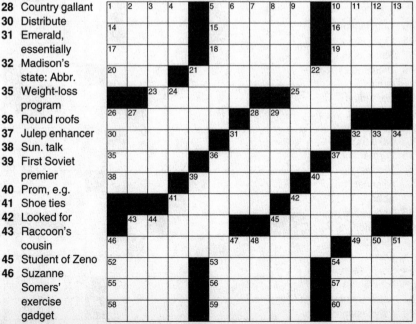

96 AT THE SYMPHONY

Rich Norris

ACROSS

1 Gone by
5 Inky smear
9 Use a razor
14 Leer at
15 Capri coin
16 Stogie
17 Sells successfully
20 Sales-kit item
21 Health farm
22 HST successor
23 Rolaids rival
25 Yale students
27 Weigh-in abbr.
30 Stadium sound
32 Throws out
36 "Uh oh!"
38 Atop
40 Come to terms
41 Engage in self-praise
44 Las Vegas area
45 China item
46 High peaks
47 Star-shaped
49 Diamond of pop music
51 Comedian Louis
52 Hit's opposite
54 Take the lead
56 Former Mideast alliance: Abbr.
58 Short snooze
60 Elevator inventor Otis
64 No __ (without conditions)
67 Actress Anouk
68 Polynesian icon
69 Do a personnel job
70 Bonnie's partner
71 Lip-balm ingredient
72 Son of Seth

DOWN

1 Places for peas
2 Taj Mahal site
3 Urban blight
4 Entice
5 Rodgers and Hart song
6 Hole edge, in golf
7 Spheres
8 Purplish gray
9 High school subj.
10 Second-guessing
11 Matured
12 Still-life subject
13 Hosp. areas
18 Musical phrase mark
19 Store event
24 Socked away
26 __ the Terrible
27 "__ luck!"
28 Rainwear
29 Show off
31 Plastic ingredient
33 Sing like Crosby
34 Towel material
35 Good judgment
37 Used a wok
39 Gift for a sweetheart
42 October birthstone
43 Requiring formal attire
48 Extended
50 Singer's syllables
53 *Ristorante* course
55 Nouveau __
56 Gas or elec.
57 Military group
59 Vessel for Jack and Jill
61 Ankle-knee connector
62 Protagonist
63 Summer drinks
64 Air Force grp.
65 Wedding-page word
66 Ring decision

97 WEATHER OR NOT

Lee Weaver

ACROSS

1 Former Iranian rulers
6 Wedding promise
9 Talons
14 Biblical prophet
15 '90s music style
16 British quart
17 In pieces
18 "We __ the World"
19 Let free
20 Flute or trumpet
23 __ Lanka
24 Swiss peak
25 Inaccurate
28 Frozen treats
31 Quality of spirit
36 Ball-game ticket stub
39 Took a chance
40 Author __ Stanley Gardner
41 Actress Verdugo
43 Low-lying islands
44 Very tart
46 Fairy-tale heroine
48 Roundabout path
50 Lift for a skier
51 __ Aviv
52 Writer Fleming
54 Domicile: Abbr.
56 President's "theme song"
64 Coiled
65 __ constrictor
66 Nairobi is its capital

67 Yard enclosure
68 __ Abner
69 Gone from one's plate
70 Wickerwork willow
71 Plumber's joint
72 Smelting residue

DOWN

1 Pygmalion playwright
2 Pueblo Indian
3 Wise __ owl
4 Flocks
5 Given to irony
6 Gershwin and Levin
7 Pub missile
8 Carmen, e.g.
9 Walked heavily
10 Bus route
11 Memo abbr.
12 Judicial order
13 Comprehend
21 Place for a statue
22 Einstein's birthplace
25 Greek nymph
26 Foolish show
27 __ mignon
29 Conger and moray
30 Aroma
32 Dashboard dial, for short
33 Characteristic
34 Philippine island
35 '50s Ford model

37 Pianist Peter
38 Door opener
42 In the know
45 Real-estate magnate
47 Destroyed
49 Scoundrel
53 Lordly
55 Clip, as wool
56 Gardener's tools
57 VW cousin
58 Picnic playwright
59 Work hard
60 Foyer
61 Division word
62 Gives a look-see
63 Rooters
64 "__ goes there?"

98 GOING UP

Rich Norris

ACROSS

1. __ Gigio (TV mouse)
5. Pre-meal prayer
10. "Quiet!"
14. Seth's son
15. Berkshire Music Festival site
16. Canton's state
17. Artful deception
20. Royal messenger
21. Plays in the pool
22. Racetrack fence
24. Portion: Abbr.
25. Goddess of plenty
28. Clark's partner
30. Hires a work force
35. Shiny mineral
37. WWII boats
39. Buzzing, as with excitement
40. One way to go out?
43. Auto supercharger
44. 28 Across portrayer
45. Choice word
46. Oration
48. Farmer's place, in song
50. Bering or Formosa: Abbr.
51. NRC predecessor
53. Hook's henchman
55. Kitchen appliances
60. Fast gait
64. Eastwood film
66. Lorre role
67. Chew the scenery
68. Composer Charles
69. Part of Q.E.D.
70. Prevent
71. Robin's residence

DOWN

1. Pianist John
2. Treater's phrase
3. Unsatisfactory
4. Actor Werner
5. Plant with sword-shaped leaves
6. Stimpy's pal
7. "No ifs, __ or buts!"
8. Provides at no cost
9. Banishes
10. __ d'oeuvres
11. "Oops!"
12. Royal honorific
13. Dan Blocker role
18. Airline to Haifa
19. Motley
23. Composer Franz
25. Leaves out
26. Photo on the wall
27. Fill with fear
29. Mrs. Peel's partner
31. Qualified
32. Puts one over on
33. Before the rest
34. More cagey
36. French cleric
38. Achy spots
41. Find
42. Multiplex attendee
47. Well-__ (wealthy)
49. Petal
52. Burglary, for one
54. Mischievous
55. Sprinter's concern
56. __ about
57. Boy or girl lead-in
58. Opportunity
59. Nose-in-the-air type
61. Not taped
62. Mine finds
63. Annoying one
65. Greek vowel

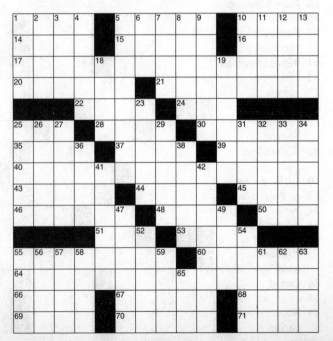

99 RIGHT DOWN YOUR ALLEY

Norma Steinberg

ACROSS

1 Turkey-stuffing herb
5 Misbehave
10 Scratch
14 Personalities
15 Actress Talia
16 "__ real nowhere man . . ."
17 Lows
18 Burn slightly
19 Terrible czar
20 Small hotel
21 Street urchin
23 Networks
25 Permit
26 Raced along
27 Frigid
32 Sultan's pride
34 Search for weapons
35 Armed conflict
36 Line of rotation
37 Feeds the pigs
38 Knight's wife
39 Sort
40 Navy and lima
41 *One Flew Over the Cuckoo's Nest* author
42 Oscar-winner for *Shampoo*
44 Mutt's pal
45 Churl
46 Egyptian stationery
49 Soda-fountain creation
54 Words in a simile
55 Skip
56 Of country life

57 Idi __
58 Actress Russo
59 Overact
60 Give temporarily
61 Leg joint
62 Plied the oars
63 Nervous

DOWN

1 18-wheelers
2 Extreme suffering
3 Stage a walkout
4 Curvy letter
5 Take for granted
6 Vouchers
7 Pale color
8 Cajole
9 Without equal

10 Glazed fabric
11 Son of Jacob
12 Memo letters
13 Diminish
21 Bacterium
22 Pursue
24 Little piggies
27 Facade
28 Torn and Van Winkle
29 Court denial
30 Nominate
31 Actor Joel
32 Sleet relative
33 Rod between wheels
34 Spanish dessert
37 Sailor
38 Stand up to
40 Cereal choice

41 Retained
43 Beard style
44 Incarcerated
46 Blue-__ special
47 Employing
48 Actress Duncan
49 Ill-fated Supreme Court nominee
50 Revival meeting cry
51 Midmorning
52 Japanese wrestling
53 Front of a boat
57 Tavern order

100 CALLING MR. FIX-IT

Lee Weaver

ACROSS

1 Heart of the matter
5 Etch or sketch
9 Shoots the breeze
13 Ancient Peruvian
14 Singer Ross
15 Birthright seller
16 Mouth-shaped garden flower
18 Actress Garr
19 Sportscaster Allen
20 Seine feeder
21 Pour, as wine
23 Delphi VIP
25 Do finger-painting
27 Cincinnati team
29 Put in order
33 Light lunch
36 Bishop of Rome
38 Crotchety one
39 Whitney and Wallach
40 Is willing to
41 Hawaiian wind
42 Mascara's target
43 Comic Johnson
44 Trigonometric functions
45 Most agile
47 Make a web
49 Combustion fluid
51 Hem material
55 Showy shrub
58 Folklore monster
60 Dinghy need
61 Microbe
62 Acrobatics performed to music

65 Sea eagle
66 Talks like Daffy Duck
67 Currency in Roma
68 Chimney residue
69 Smooth the way
70 Finished the cake

DOWN

1 Thingamabob
2 More private
3 La __ Opera House
4 Beer-keg adjunct
5 Cape of Good Hope explorer
6 Current crazes
7 Pitch __-hitter
8 Roamed about
9 Begin work
10 Toward the ocean
11 Silo's neighbor
12 Look good on
14 Helped with the dishes
17 Parceled (out)
22 Corn unit
24 Auto racer's headgear
26 Sugar sources
28 Very dapper
30 Lunch time for some
31 Left
32 Greek vowels
33 Do a clerk's job
34 Jai __
35 Santa's reminder

37 Three-strikes result
40 Like drip-dry material
44 __ with (supported)
46 Summer: Fr.
48 Job-related extras
50 Rich soil deposit
52 Greek column type
53 Mother-of-pearl
54 Midas' undoing
55 A long time
56 Zilch
57 Florence's river
59 Stare agog
63 River inlet
64 Poetic pugilist

ANSWERS

1

```
MASS  ESS   LOTS
DANCE UTAH  INRE
ONTOP PALO  STEN
COINAPHRASE  HAS
    CLEO DEPLETE
MACE  ARMS  IAM
EVAS  CIA SCOOPS
NOS CHANGES  NEA
UNHOLY  SRA PEEL
  ELI BEER  RYNE
MADEFOR  ACRE
ALI FOOTTHEBILL
DINE  PLIE  BASIE
ANON  SINS EKING
MEND  NET   LEST
```

2

```
OPED  GAMAL  PLOT
RATE  OCALA  RIPE
TRAFFICJAM  ELIA
SALIENT  MEISTER
   LAG  AORTA
RAWER  ENS AGLET
ANI   EGG SLEEVE
JELLYROLLMORTON
ANDEAN  EVA  UKE
STEEL  TRI ASSET
  SIDES  SMU
HASBEEN  UTENSIL
ETTU BUTTERUPTO
STAR ARIEL  PEEN
SANG REESE  SEMI
```

3

```
SAP  POLARIS  COP
AMO  ANAPEST  ALI
UPPERCIRCLE  TEX
NELLIE   TETRA
ARABS EGOS  OPEC
SERE  TBAR  BLUSH
  IRAN ORELSE
STICKINGPLASTER
CANOES  WALT
ALTOS MAYA  PARS
MEET  BAYS BEGET
  REELS  GREENE
LIV FACEFLANNEL
ALA ODOROUS  TEA
GEL RETAPES  SSE
```

4

```
TATA  ROTC PROAM
ARIA  OKRA EARLE
MONA  MAINSTREET
PAP  APATITE
ARACHNID GISTS
NAYS  ISNT  OED
PLAID UCLA  ABLE
ILLNESS  ALABAMA
COLE  IAMB FOCAL
AYE  INFO  MARC
  DYING OVERTONE
  CULPRIT  RAD
MEMORYLANE  BORG
ALONE  AGER  RACE
GLOSS  NESS  ODOR
```

5

```
ARIA  BALSA  DAFT
LODI  ALIEN  OBOE
BOER  SLEEK  TEEN
FASHIONPLATES
  PONY   EPI
SETAT  SAD  REHAB
ALICES  ERA  ORA
SATELLITEDISHES
ETA  YON  ASTUTE
SENSE  NAT  AIMED
  ALA  EGAL
FLYINGSAUCERS
CEES  GOOSE  TATA
PENN  LOSES  TIED
ASTO  ODORS  ONTO
```

6

```
SRIS  DALE  PERCE
TENT  EVIL  ALIAS
ALBA  TORA  NESTS
GEORGEWALLACE
SEXIER   OCT
  NORMANTHOMAS
HOT  LEICA  ERASE
AHEM  DRAMA  SLEW
DICOT  EGEST  IAN
JOHNANDERSON
  ERE   ARABIA
  STROMTHURMOND
GENII  ORAL  AGRA
AGAZE  PINT  TEEM
LOPED  EGGS  HYDE
```

7

```
AHOY  SWAP   ZAP
MOVE  MARES  PALE
PRESSAGENT  ISLE
SAN  PRES  ANNUAL
  SETS  CROC
SASHAY  HOTSHOTS
CLERK  DOPE  PROW
RAVI  PAPER  ELLE
AMEN  OVID  GNOME
PORKLOIN  BONNET
  WORD  GAMY
GEORGE  PERE  ODE
ALMA  SQUEEZEBOX
WEEP  TUSKS  NOWI
KEN   ASST  DENT
```

8

```
EDER  RESEE   BEL
MERE  EVENS  PERE
SELF  TENDS  RENE
DEEPEN  SERENER
   REST   NEZ
RESENT  PRECEPTS
ELLEN  FEES  SEEP
EVE   REN   TRE
SEWS  SEPT  MEESE
ESSENCES  FESSED
  EER   BENT
SLEDDED  REDEEM
PEPE  EELED  ELEE
EWER  CLEVE  METS
CDE   HEXER  SMEE
```

9

```
CODA  GRASP  WEST
ODIN  LUGER  RIPE
BORN  ENERO  ORAL
BREADANDBUTTER
      AMY   DIE
LILACS KEEP  SNL
IRISH IANS  STOA
MEATANDPOTATOES
INRI  ALPS  DARNS
TES   AREA  LAREDO
      ERR   SON
MILKANDCOOKIES
ZERO  TAROT ADZE
ASAP  ETAPE HERA
PANE  DOMED NEAT
```

10

```
ROSS  RECAP  SWAB
OGEE  AGATE  PIPE
DRAWINGPAD  ADES
EER  STEP  ARREST
     SLED  SLOTS
HASHED  COLLAPSE
ASHES  TOWEL  RCA
LIED  CAVED  SEAS
ODE  LONER  SHALE
SETTINGS  SHADES
     MUSTY  CHOW
SHERPA  ERIE  SEE
MATT  COVERSTORY
URAL  TWEET  AFAR
TILE  SENDS  BASE
```

11

```
SALE  DARK   SWAP
LRON  ELENA  TONI
AGRI  LODES  ANTE
CURDSANDWHEY
KEY  ENG   AERIE
     SNOWS  ARDENS
ASSET  ITAL  PUT
THEWAYTOSANJOSE
PIA  AHAS  OASES
ANTHEM  TERRY
RESET  SAM  VMI
     WEIGHSTATION
JIVE  ZEROS  MOPS
OVER  ENERO  ELEE
GETS  ASSN   NAST
```

12

```
PICT  BLAB   TOMB
ECHO  EARL   OPERA
PEAL  ANNO   UTTER
SPLITDECISIONS
RES    SLO
REPLAN  SPLENDOR
ARIOT  TORI  RBI
MATTEROFOPINION
OTO  ENTS  CAVES
SONNYBOY  CHEESE
EAU   ELO
SILENTMAJORITY
ABASK  AGES  NOUS
CANOE  PUCE  COLA
REND   SETS  ALEX
```

13

```
TEA  BARNUM  SERF
ORS  AROUSE  ALIE
NIP  NICKELPLATE
ACE  DOSES  LANES
LANAIS    MOM
     STOPONADIME
AIMS  LIARS  OAR
WREN  BULBS  LOSE
NAN  CAMEO  UNTO
QUARTERBACK
GOT    POETIC
ALIEN  SPAIN  ODA
PENNYLOAFER  TAR
ENID  ALPACA  AHA
DATA  SOARED  LOT
```

14

```
ASS  ROAST  SLITS
NIT  ENVOY  IOWAS
IRA  STEPPINGOUT
TENET  HEMA
ANDROID  RATTRAP
INROAD  TROUPE
SON  ENROL  ANNIE
TAGS  SENAT  SNAP
ASPEN  ROTOR  INS
GEARED  REBORN
ESTATES  RENEGES
     TRIO  ASWAN
WALKINGTALL  ITO
ALVIN  HOPED  LEW
SLING  TEENS  DRY
```

15

```
 CCC   HUD   PASTA
BLAH  SATE  ACMES
EINE  ELAN  THATS
SQUARESHOOTER
TUTTUT  THY  TAC
SEE  CHAFES  FIXE
     AKELA  WINED
BERMUDATRIANGLE
OREOS  HUMPS
TONK  SCAMPI  SUB
HOO  SUR  ATTUNE
VICIOUSCIRCLE
DRACO  CLOT  ICER
ROTOR  UNIS  NOSY
SCENE  SAL   IRS
```

16

```
USGA  TAPS  RECAP
NEIL  AREA  ENLAI
FILECLERK  START
ENDURE  MISTIMES
DESTINES  CORP
     ITTY  LAREDO
ALFA  SEMITE  ORO
VEINS  LAS  SAWER
EAR  TAINTS  SNOB
REMIND  ETAS
DEPT  ADELAIDE
STRAPSON  LAUDED
TRILL  MAILPLANE
BELIE  NINA  THEN
DELED  ISAR  SOBS
```

17

```
APORT  SCAR  CASA
NAMER  OHIO  OREL
GUNBARRELS  MEAL
ELI  LETS  CLEARS
LASSES  SCOUT
     HEEP  REMOVES
LALA  TAKE  EGADI
AMIDE  LED  TRIED
SODOM  ENID  INNS
TROWELS  TEMP
     BEATS  BASALT
REBORN  PAID  REA
ALEX  COURTCASES
MILE  ETRE  ABORT
PETS  ROSS  PANSY
```

18

```
ASH   MICAS  LSAT
DOOR  AROMA  ELIE
ALOE  HOOPDREAMS
RELEARNS  SOCKET
ISLES  ETCHERS
BAGELS  BLAKE
LHASA  CELT  SHEA
USN  HOOSIER  OAR
ROSS  NETS  ILOVE
     HEEDS  STAVES
ESCORTS  SPACE
THRONE  AIRSTRIP
HOOTENANNY  IDOL
ANNE  TRACE  CANE
NEER  HATER  MAD
```

19

```
ABBE  ODESSA  JOT
SEAT  LEEANN  OLE
KATEJACKSON  HEX
THRONE  HOEING
NADIR  PARD
REGAN  TET  LEER
APULIA  TOE  SNUB
JAY  EMERALD  VIA
ACME  OVA  SEVENS
TAMP  ACC  SERGE
DUAD  ELFIN
HISSES  OILIER
GIS  TRACYAUSTIN
ADO  AMULET  ONIT
YEN  SOLIDS  NASH
```

20

```
CASH  CHIN  UTAHN
OCTO  HINT  PALAU
CHICKENCHOWMEIN
AER  ASEA  PAPERS
     ARTS  SIRS
GENRES  DUAD  EFT
ATONE  OAST  ALAI
SHRIMPFRIEDRICE
EAVE  ETTE  OTTER
SNO  TEES  SLEETS
     HAWN  TELL
PLEASE  SACO  AVE
LOBSTERCHOPSUEY
ELATE  NOON  ARTE
DANES  AWED  MASS
```

21

H I H I	■	R E R U N	■ G O E S

```
H I H I ■ R E R U N ■ G O E S
I T A L ■ O M E G A ■ L I L T
P H I L O S O P H I C A L L Y
S E R ■ N I T S ■ S U S S E X
■ ■ ■ A D E E ■ A M E S ■ ■ ■
B A S K E R ■ A M I S ■ H A L
O P T I C ■ S M I T ■ S O M E
T H I N K S N O T H I N G O F
H I E S ■ W A R Y ■ L E A N T
A D S ■ G E R E ■ S L A N G Y
■ ■ ■ F L A K ■ R E I D ■ ■ ■
A R M O U R ■ C A A N ■ A L A
C H I N E S E H I B I S C U S
T E N D ■ I N U S E ■ K I R K
S E G A ■ N A M E D ■ I D E S
```

22

```
B A L D ■ P A R A ■ G A V I N
A F O R ■ O M A R ■ O N I C E
C R E A M P U F F ■ B Y L A W
H O W W I L L ■ ■ A D A M S ■
■ ■ ■ D I E T S ■ C A S E Y ■
■ P I E I N T H E S K Y ■ ■ ■
S O A R ■ ■ E A S T ■ ■ P T A
S U G A R R A Y L E O N A R D
S R O ■ ■ E A R S ■ ■ B R E D
■ ■ ■ P I E C E O F C A K E ■
■ B J O R N ■ H E L L O ■ ■ ■
L U R I D ■ ■ D U N G E O N ■
A L I N E ■ J O H N C A N D Y
S I N C E ■ F L A K ■ I V E S
E A G E R ■ K A T Y ■ L Y R E
```

23

```
I T E M ■ S C A R F ■ A K I N
T E L E ■ L U N A R ■ D I N E
H E A D F O R T H E H I L L S
O T T ■ R O L E ■ Q U O T A S
■ T H E P I P S ■ B U N S ■ ■
E D S ■ ■ T R E K ■ ■ C A P ■
A T S E A ■ S O O N ■ D U L Y
B E L L Y U P T O T H E B A R
L A O S ■ L O U D ■ O B E S E
■ E S T ■ ■ S T O P ■ ■ M O I
■ ■ G A I N ■ C A P T I V E ■
I D R E A M ■ F O U L ■ L E A
F O O T B A L L P L A Y E R S
A D A M ■ T E A S E ■ E D G E
T O N E ■ E N T E R ■ S E E D
```

24

```
E R A S ■ W I P E R ■ T A S S
R O L E ■ A S I D E ■ A L A I
S U P P L Y A N D D E M A N D
T E S T I F Y ■ S I A M E S E
■ ■ ■ U N A ■ A R Y ■ ■ ■ ■ ■
C O M M E R C I A L P A P E R
A T A ■ E R N S ■ N I C E ■ ■
S A R A ■ R O T H S ■ D E L I
■ ■ A R I L ■ P R E P ■ R A N
S Y S T E M S A N A L Y S T S
■ ■ ■ ■ R T E ■ C E O ■ ■ ■ ■
A S S U A G E ■ R E A G E N T
D I G I T A L C O M P U T E R
A N T S ■ L L A M A ■ R U L E
M O S T ■ O A T E N ■ T I L E
```

25

```
S A Y A ■ A M I S ■ M O C H A
A T O M ■ G E O L ■ A R E A S
M A Y O R E D W A R D K O C H
S N O R E ■ I N N E R ■ S K Y
■ ■ ■ A T T A ■ G E E S ■ ■ ■
W I L L I E M A Y S ■ U S N A
A L I ■ T E E N ■ E D I T O R
T O N A L ■ N T S ■ I T O L D
E V E N E D ■ I T E M ■ R I O
R E N D ■ O S C A R M A Y E R
■ ■ ■ C O P A ■ R E E L ■ ■ ■
M O M ■ H E L O T ■ S O L T I
T H E M A Y O B R O T H E R S
S O R E R ■ M I E N ■ A C U T
T H E T A ■ E E K S ■ S H E S
```

26

```
L O D E ■ T R I A D ■ S L O T
E B O N ■ A B O V E ■ E E R O
F O W L ■ M I D I S ■ A T N O
T E N A M ■ O V E R L O O K ■
■ ■ ■ W I N D O W ■ R O A N ■
D D E ■ O R I N ■ T U N E U P
R O N ■ P U L I ■ T E S T Y ■
A N T S ■ M Y N A H ■ S H U L
M O M M A ■ G R A B ■ A R E ■
A T C O S T ■ S I Z E ■ I N S
■ G O T A ■ T A Y L O R ■ ■ ■
T R I C O L O R ■ G O D O T ■
M I N H ■ E V E R T ■ O O N A
E T T E ■ S E E T O ■ O W E R
N A Y S ■ E N T E R ■ O N A N
```

27

```
T I F F S ■ P A R I S ■ D E S
A L L A T ■ A M E B A ■ A M T
G L A D A L L O V E R ■ I C E
■ ■ ■ T I E R ■ ■ A T S E A ■
C A R O L E R ■ R E L A Y E D
A N O D E S ■ K A R E E M ■ ■
R I S E R ■ F A V R E ■ I M P
R T E S ■ B A R E S ■ C L I O
Y A K ■ H A V E N ■ P O L L S
■ ■ E D I S O N ■ S E R E N E
H A N D L E R ■ C H E E R E D
A R N E L ■ P A A R ■ ■ ■ ■ ■
I L E ■ M U M S T H E W O R D
F E D ■ A M I S H ■ S O F A R
A N Y ■ N A S T Y ■ S O F T Y
```

28

```
M A D E ■ M I S T ■ F O N T S
O P A L ■ A C M E ■ E M E R Y
S A L E S R O O M ■ M A X I M
S T I C K I N G P O I N T S ■
■ ■ ■ T E A ■ I N N ■ ■ ■ ■ ■
R A G ■ E C H O ■ S I T S I N
E R L E ■ H A R E ■ S E I N E
T O U C H I N G R E M A R K S
A S T R A ■ D A M A ■ M E E T
R E S U L T ■ N A R C ■ D R S
■ ■ ■ ■ Y E S ■ T O P ■ ■ ■ ■
■ A T T A C H E D H O U S E S
S L Y E R ■ E X E M P L A R Y
H I R E D ■ B A L E ■ S H I N
E T O N S ■ A M E N ■ E L K E
```

29

```
A C T ■ S P E E D S ■ P E R P
L E O ■ P O L L O I ■ A Q U A
L A S ■ U N S U N G ■ P U T S
O S C A R D E L A H O Y A ■ ■
Y E A S T ■ ■ ■ T A R T A R ■
■ ■ ■ H O O V E R ■ S U I T E
G A B ■ U N I T E S ■ S O O N
E R E ■ T O N Y D O W ■ N N E
N Y E S ■ S I M I L E ■ S E W
O A K U M ■ C A D E T S ■ ■ ■
■ A N E M I C ■ ■ ■ L I E G E
■ ■ E M M Y L O U H A R R I S
R E P O ■ R E A S O N ■ O J S
O X E N ■ I N T E N D ■ D O E
T O R S ■ L A S S E S ■ E E N
```

30

```
D O N H O ■ N E R F ■ A C T S
A D I O S ■ O V A L ■ S H A M
R E N T S T R I K E ■ T A X I
■ ■ L I U ■ L E X ■ O R E L ■
A C H I E S T ■ R E P R I S E
C H A N ■ S R A ■ D O I T ■ ■
R I C E ■ L A S H ■ P A Y U P
E L K ■ Z E P H Y R S ■ B R O
S E I N E ■ P E P E ■ W A G S
■ ■ N E A R ■ N E V ■ A L E S
H A G G L E D ■ D E W I L D E
A L F A ■ D O C ■ R A T ■ ■ ■
R O O T ■ C O U N T Y F A I R
S H U E ■ A N T E ■ N O I S E
H A L S ■ P E S T ■ E R R O L
```

31

```
M O A T ■ S C A R ■ M A S H
O P R A H ■ H O B O ■ I L K A
M E C C A ■ A C E S ■ G A I N
■ C H O C O L A T E C H I P S
■ ■ ■ ■ K A T ■ M A T ■ ■ ■ ■
G A M E S T ■ A F A R ■ A H A
O P E R A ■ F A I R ■ I R O N
S T R A W B E R R Y B L O N D
E E L S ■ A T O M ■ E L M E R
E R E ■ S C A N ■ D E S A D E
■ ■ ■ ■ O A K ■ E A T ■ ■ ■ ■
V A N I L L A E X T R A C T ■
E R I N ■ A B L E ■ E T H E R
T I C K ■ S O I R ■ D I A N A
O D E S ■ H O S T ■ T R O Y
```

32

```
H O F F A ■ O M O O ■ P A B A
A L E A N ■ W O N T ■ A D A M
T E R R Y C L O T H ■ T A L E
S O N A T A ■ R O E N T G E N
■ ■ ■ ■ D I N S ■ P R A Y E R S
A M I ■ M A T ■ ■ ■ S I C ■ ■
B O O M E R A N G ■ L A Y O N
C A T O ■ D R O O D ■ K A N E
S T A L K ■ S N O R K E L E R
■ ■ L E T ■ ■ ■ F I N ■ L S D
S A W Y E R S ■ S P E D ■ ■ ■
C R A B L I K E ■ P E R S I A
A R L O ■ P E N N Y C A N D Y
D O L L ■ L E D A ■ A M I L E
S W A T ■ E T O N ■ P A T E S
```

33

```
APAT  DACCA  SPAN
DISH  INOIL  ARMY
ONCEINABLUEMOON
STORMS  RIMA  FRY
  STEP  DAUNTS
    ORO  MASCARA
MAHARAJA  AHAS
AMONTHOFSUNDAYS
TOOT  TAKESTEN
ASPECTS  YES
  DARERS  TOMS
HEM  RENO  AERATE
EVERYNOWANDTHEN
LIME  DREAD  HAVE
PLOD  SARAH  OLES
```

34

```
SAYS  ABES  DRAB
PLEAT  MORE  ROSE
OLLIE  BURR  ACHE
OILSPILL  GAWKER
LEO  ILED  IPSO
   WEDS  EFOR  FRO
UPSA  ACRE  ORGAN
TETRA  ACE  NAIVE
ALONG  GOLF  CBER
HEN  NOEL  ICER
  EDEN  OPAL  ASI
IMPISH  RETITLED
NEAP  ABAT  MOTEL
MARS  NODE  BLAME
ELKO  DOOR  DRED
```

35

```
DIET  CHRIS  SNUG
ANNA  HENNA  TOLL
BACKTOBACK  ASTO
STEERS  HEATERS
  SEETHE  RITAS
SOFAS  BOD  LOO
ONA  SPAS  BONNET
BUCO  ARABY  SODA
SPENDS  NOES  SIP
  TEE  ONO  ABETS
GOOSE  CABANA
ONFIRST  SYSTEM
LEAD  HANDTOHAND
FACE  ONAIR  EROS
SLED  TEMPO  SASE
```

36

```
ASAN  OPEN  BARK
SOLO  SEAN  RUPEE
FAIRSHARE  IRONY
AVE  TACT  AGREES
RENTA  HOTSHOT
  OKAY  ACTS
JETSET  ERRS  DIP
ALAS  ROSSI  TORE
MIX  POST  BARCAR
  SAPS  PESO
  SKYHIGH  IDOLS
FRAIDY  AIDA  HAM
AETNA  PLAINJANE
SPINY  ELLS  ORAL
TONY  POSH  BAIT
```

37

```
TOILS  SHOE  CAPP
ABOUT  TEUT  OREO
BOWLEROFTHEYEAR
SEALION  RELEASE
   ANTE  ALLS
SERB  SAG  TOOT
CRAYON  NECK  XVI
RAY  RESIDUE  BAR
USO  BEAT  ZYGOTE
BENE  NAH  OWED
  ROAM  ASAP
AMERICA  REDHEAD
DEMOLITIONDERBY
ICER  NELL  TRIBE
THUS  GOLD  OSCAR
```

38

```
TOGAS  TOMS  AWES
ERASE  ARAT  CHAT
MOTHERMAYI  TOTE
  ISE  LAFF  SEW
THERES  SLIPON
POOREST  ETON
RAW  DEALT  SOFAS
ELMO  STORE  PITA
PLUMP  STIES  RRS
  COIL  ELAPSES
PHONES  DEVOTE
MAW  TECH  ROT
EROO  WHATSUPDOC
STOW  AMSO  RIOTS
HYDE  YOHO  SENTA
```

39

```
  LAB  STICH  ABCS
COMO  TAMPA  VIAL
ICESTATIONZEBRA
AIRCADET  DORSEY
    SIR  GYNT
MICASA  TOME  VIM
ANOSE  TUBA  SONY
MCMILLANANDWIFE
BUBS  AXED  EELER
ORO  AYES  CLEARS
  ATAD  SAR
AVEDON  DORISDAY
SENDMENOFLOWERS
PACE  GOTTO  ABEL
SLED  GUEST  PIA
```

40

```
SMA  SEMI  ELMS
CORSAGES  ACQUIT
ROLLCALL  BRUISE
AREA  DDE  HOISTS
PESTO  STOP
  SVC  ARCADES
FRO  AARON  IRANI
REVOLVINGCREDIT
ONENO  STOIC  ADE
GIRAFFE  ALT
  FARM  ERECT
SKIPIT  OAR  AMOR
PALACE  SPINCITY
ANKLES  SECRETES
NESS  OSHA  SST
```

41

```
AMOS  BABAS  SELA
LISI  OVERT  PRIG
ASHE  BARNEYFIFE
SCARAB  GORE  KEN
  RUY  ELGART
BRIANPICCOLO
EAR  TIMOR  SOAPS
ETAL  NAMES  NERO
SENOR  MEETS  ROB
  WHISTLESTOPS
CURSOR  AGA
UNO  DIRE  MTHOOD
FLUTEDEDGE  IRMA
FIGS  INNER  TEED
STEP  COALS  IONS
```

42

```
APEG  BLOW  GLATT
NOLO  RICO  PIQUE
DOLLARSTODONUTS
CRAFT  TIDE  EAST
  LIPS  LABS
SPRITE  CARR  OBS
OLAN  PLAN  ASSET
HECKLEANDJECKLE
OBESE  DOSE  AAAA
TED  CHIN  DARRYL
  RHUE  RICE
AHAH  RSTU  DCLII
SOCIALDEMOCRATS
PLANE  AMOR  OUZO
SENOR  YARD  WEAR
```

43

```
OPALS  SACK  KATE
RELIT  ONOR  ELAL
GETSOFFTHETRACK
SKILLET  EBONITE
  EARN  RST
THIS  ESE  ABAR
HEM  LISP  MALONE
EXPRESSOPINIONS
TEEHEE  ORLY  NEO
ARLO  TKO  SEED
  UTE  BABE
SAFFRON  ASOCIAL
TRAINSOFTHOUGHT
ARID  ERIE  BROAD
BARE  ESTD  SETHS
```

44

```
MAAM  MASC  BEDS
UCLA  PINTO  AQUA
STUN  ASKER  TUTU
  MOUNTAINCHAIN
BAIRNS  NBA  TEA
ANN  CYAN  ACCESS
HAUL  RIALTO
  MISSINGLINK
SEEDER  SHAM
BEHAVE  SALT  OWE
ERE  ESS  ENAMEL
WASONTHEFENCE
ASTA  OATER  HIFI
REEK  IRONY  ENOS
ERRS  TEND  DIET
```

45

H	O	N	S		A	S	I	F		I	T	E	M	S
E	R	I	C		L	E	N	A		M	I	X	E	S
R	I	T	E		T	A	C	K		B	E	T	T	E
D	O	W	N	T	O	T	H	E	W	I	R	E		
E	L	I	T	E				D	A	B		R	A	F
D	E	T		M	O	C	K		S	E	A	N	C	E
			A	P	R	O	N	S			R	A	R	E
E	M	O	T	I	O	N	A	L	O	U	T	L	E	T
R	A	V	I			S	C	O	O	T	S			
S	K	E	T	C	H		K	E	P	T		S	H	A
E	E	R		L	A	S			E	T	H	I	C	
	S	T	A	Y	E	D	C	U	R	R	E	N	T	
T	R	I	O	S		W	A	R	P		E	R	G	O
O	O	Z	E	S		E	R	O	S		A	P	E	R
N	E	E	D	Y		D	E	W	Y		D	A	D	S

46

B	E	L	T		R	I	S	E	R		A	S	P	S
A	R	I	A		U	N	C	L	E		M	U	L	E
B	A	S	K	E	T	C	A	S	E		E	P	E	E
A	S	T	E	R		A	R	I	D		L	E	A	K
R	E	S	O	R	T			Y	E	S	S	I	R	
				U	S	E	D			H	A	B	I	T
D	U	C	T		N	U	A	N	C	E		O	D	E
I	C	H		C	O	P	I	E	R	S		W	E	E
A	L	E		O	R	E	L	S	E		C	L	A	N
L	A	S	T	S				T	A	C	O			
	T	A	T	T	L	E			M	O	L	E	S	T
A	R	C	S		H	A	L	F		B	L	A	K	E
R	O	O	T		R	I	V	E	R	B	A	S	I	N
I	D	L	E		O	N	E	T	O		G	E	L	S
Z	E	D	S		B	E	S	E	T		E	L	L	E

47

A	B	O	M	B		A	S	I	A		A	G	O	G
T	A	U	P	E		C	O	L	D		M	I	M	E
O	N	T	H	E	W	H	O	L	E		O	V	A	L
M	D	S		L	I	O	N		Q	U	E	E	N	S
			T	I	T	O		J	U	M	B	O		
S	I	M	O	N	S		T	E	A	P	A	R	T	Y
C	N	O	T	E		M	A	S	T	S		T	I	E
A	F	R	O		V	E	R	S	E		M	A	M	A
L	E	E		D	E	E	R	E		C	A	K	E	S
P	R	O	P	E	R	T	Y		P	R	I	E	S	T
			R	I	F	T	S		L	O	U	D		
P	I	L	A	T	E		N	I	N	E		G	O	P
E	D	E	N		B	Y	A	N	D	L	A	R	G	E
A	L	S	O		R	A	Z	E			E	X	I	L	E
T	E	S	S		A	K	I	N		R	E	P	E	L

48

T	A	B	S		T	A	P	I	R		B	A	R	D
U	B	E	T		A	B	A	T	E		E	R	I	E
B	O	L	A		T	A	R	A	S		E	L	L	E
B	U	L	L	F	I	D	D	L	E		F	O	L	D
S	T	Y	L	I				O	A	F	S			
			S	L	I	M	S			L	A	T	V	I	A
A	T	A		E	M	A	I	L		N	E	O	N	S
B	A	L	O	N	E	Y	S	A	N	D	W	I	C	H
C	L	A	R	A		S	A	M	B	A		D	A	Y
S	C	R	A	M	S			L	E	A	N	T		
			N	E	A	T			G	R	U	M	P	
S	L	U	G		B	U	N	K	H	O	U	S	E	S
T	A	X	I		E	L	E	N	A		M	E	S	A
A	V	O	N			R	I	V	E	R		P	U	T	T
B	A	R	A		S	P	E	E	D		S	P	A	S

49

A	H	O	Y		S	W	A	N			Z	A	P	
M	O	V	E		M	A	R	I	S		P	A	L	E
P	R	E	S	S	A	G	E	N	T		I	S	L	E
S	A	N		P	R	E	S		A	N	N	U	A	L
			S	E	T	S		C	R	O	C			
S	A	S	H	A	Y		H	O	T	S	H	O	T	S
C	L	E	R	K		D	O	P	E		P	R	O	W
R	A	V	I		P	A	P	E	R		E	T	R	E
A	M	E	N		O	V	I	D		G	N	O	M	E
P	O	R	K	L	O	I	N		B	O	N	N	E	T
			W	O	R	D		G	A	M	Y			
G	E	O	R	G	E		P	E	R	E		O	D	E
A	L	M	A		S	Q	U	E	E	Z	E	B	O	X
W	E	E	P		T	U	S	K	S		N	O	W	I
K	E	N			A	S	S	T		D	E	N	T	

50

D	A	N	A		C	E	D	A	R		A	F	A	R
O	R	E	S		A	D	A	G	E		P	O	P	E
F	I	S	H	I	N	G	R	O	D		P	O	S	E
F	A	S		M	I	E	N			D	I	E	T	E	D
			S	A	N	D		L	E	G	A	L		
V	O	Y	A	G	E		H	O	N	O	R	I	N	G
O	V	A	T	E		R	I	S	E	R		G	O	A
T	I	R	E		C	A	K	E	D		T	H	E	M
E	N	D		G	O	N	E	R		T	I	T	L	E
D	E	M	U	R	R	E	R		D	R	E	S	S	Y
			A	N	I	S	E		B	A	U	D		
P	E	S	E	T	A		M	A	I	L		A	D	S
E	T	T	A		G	R	A	N	N	Y	K	N	O	T
O	N	E	S		E	C	L	A	T		O	K	R	A
N	A	R	Y		S	A	L	L	Y		A	H	A	B

51

S	H	O	W		M	A	M	E		C	O	B	R	A
T	U	N	A		A	W	A	Y		U	R	I	E	L
A	L	I	T		Y	A	L	E		R	A	N	G	E
R	A	N	C	H	D	R	E	S	S	I	N	G		
			H	E	A	D			C	O	G			
T	A	W	D	R	Y		B	R	A		S	E	W	N
I	D	I	O	M		S	L	I	M	S		V	I	A
L	O	D	G	E	A	C	O	M	P	L	A	I	N	T
E	R	E		S	P	A	N	S		E	N	A	C	T
D	E	N	S		A	N	D		J	I	T	N	E	Y
			C	A	R		M	A	G	I				
	C	O	T	T	A	G	E	C	H	E	E	S	E	
A	T	O	L	L		L	E	E	K		T	I	E	R
P	A	N	D	A		P	A	S	A		A	R	E	A
T	R	E	S	S		O	R	E	L		M	E	S	S

52

F	A	N	S		T	S	A	R		D	A	U	B	S
O	P	A	L		I	T	N	O		I	G	L	O	O
O	R	S	O		M	A	N	A		S	N	E	A	D
L	I	T	T	L	E	I	O	D	I	N	E			
S	L	Y		A	T	R	Y		N	E	W	M	A	N
			S	N	O	W		S	T	Y		O	N	O
A	L	C	O	A		E	C	H	O		A	N	T	S
W	E	E	W	I	L	L	I	E	W	I	N	K	I	E
A	N	D	S		E	L	I	E		M	E	S	S	Y
I	T	E		W	A	S		T	H	A	W			
T	O	S	S	E	S		S	M	O	G		A	S	K
			P	E	E	W	E	E	H	E	R	M	A	N
D	E	R	E	K		O	P	T	O		U	P	T	O
A	T	A	L	L		U	T	A	H		S	L	O	W
M	A	N	L	Y		K	I	L	O			H	E	N	S

53

R	A	P	T		H	E	R	O	D		R	A	F	T
U	S	E	R		O	L	I	V	E		U	L	A	N
N	O	R	A		S	E	V	E	N		P	I	T	T
	F	I	N	N	E	G	A	N	S	W	A	K	E	
			Q	U	A	Y				H	U	E	D	
K	A	P	U	T			C	I	V	I	L			
E	S	A	I		A	V	A	T	A	R		W	E	E
G	I	L	L	I	G	A	N	S	I	S	L	A	N	D
S	A	M		V	E	S	T	A	L		A	D	O	G
			H	A	D	T	O		O	B	E	S	E	
S	O	O	N			C	A	R	R					
M	C	N	A	M	A	R	A	S	B	A	N	D		
R	I	T	E		A	L	I	B	I		D	E	E	P
A	L	E	S		T	E	P	I	D		O	M	A	R
J	E	T	T		S	C	E	N	E		R	O	R	Y

54

A	Q	A	B	A		B	I	C	S		S	H	O	P
L	U	N	A	S		A	C	H	E		H	A	L	O
L	I	N	T	S	C	R	E	E	N		O	L	D	S
			H	E	A	D	S	F	O	R		L	I	E
R	E	S	E	T	S				R	A	M	M	E	D
E	L	K	S		T	E	S	S		G	E	O		
A	L	E		G	E	N	I	I		T	O	N	E	R
M	I	L	E	R		A	L	T		A	N	I	M	A
S	E	E	T	O		C	L	A	N	G		T	E	T
			T	A	P		T	Y	R	O		S	O	N	S
C	H	O	L	E	R				H	A	I	R	D	O
I	A	N			D	A	Y	S	H	I	F	T		
N	I	K	E		P	O	T	A	T	O	C	H	I	P
C	L	E	M		I	R	A	N		R	O	U	T	E
H	E	Y	S		D	E	B	S		E	M	B	E	R

55

C	R	A	M		C	E	D	A	R		S	C	A	M
R	O	V	E		I	R	A	T	E		O	O	P	S
A	G	A	R		N	O	M	A	D		U	K	E	S
B	U	S	I	N	E	S	S	L	E	T	T	E	R	
S	E	T	T	E	R			L	A	S	H			
			S	T	A	M	P		L	A	P	S	E	S
A	N	E		M	A	R	S			R	A	T	I	O
T	A	K	E	S	A	T	O	N	E	S	W	O	R	D
O	N	E	T	O		A	S	A	N			P	E	A
M	U	S	C	L	E		E	G	G	O	N			
			H	O	R	A		I	C	E	S	U	P	
P	R	I	S	O	N	S	E	N	T	E	N	C	E	
A	L	A	N		T	I	L	D	E		D	O	O	R
S	A	N	G		I	M	A	G	E		E	R	N	O
I	N	K	S		C	A	P	E	R			D	E	N	T

56

E	D	A	M		J	E	D	I		W	H	E	L	P
L	I	M	A		E	X	A	M		R	A	D	I	O
H	O	O	K	E	D	O	N	P	H	O	N	I	C	S
I	N	R	E	M		G	R	I	T		N	I	T	
			M	A	S	K		O	V	E	R	A	T	E
L	I	N	E	I	T	E	M	V	E	T	O			
A	B	A		L	O	N	E			O	O	Z	E	S
M	A	R	L		W	O	L	F	E			K	I	L	L
P	R	Y	O	R		T	E	N	S		T	I	E	
			W	O	R	M	S	E	Y	E	V	I	E	W
L	O	R	E	L	E	I			D	A	T	A		
A	M	I		A	I	D	S			I	N	A	N	E
C	A	S	T	I	N	G	O	U	T	N	I	N	E	S
K	N	E	A	D		E	L	M	O		S	N	A	P
S	I	N	U	S		T	O	A	T			H	O	R	N

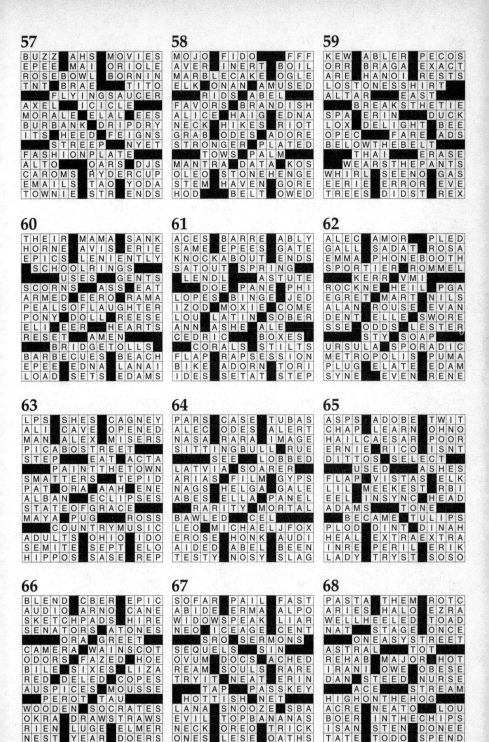

57

```
BUZZ  AHS   MOVIES
EPEE  MAI   ORIOLE
ROSEBOWL    BORNIN
TNT   BRAE    TITO
  FLYINGSAUCER
AXEL    ICICLE
MORALE  ELAL   EES
BURBANK  DRIPDRY
ITS  HEED  FEIGNS
   STREEP   NYET
FASHIONPLATE
ALTO   OARS   DJS
CAROMS  RYDERCUP
EMAILS  TAO   YODA
TOWNIE  STR   ENDS
```

58

```
MOJO  FIDO     FFF
AVER  INERT   BOIL
MARBLECAKE    OGLE
ELK  ONAN  AMUSED
       RIDS  ABEL
FAVORS   BRANDISH
ALICE  HAIG   EDNA
NECK  HIKES   RIOT
GRAB  ODES   ADORE
STRONGER   PLATED
     TOWS   PALM
MANTRA  DATA   KOS
OLEO  STONEHENGE
STEM  HAVEN   GORE
HOD    BELT   OWED
```

59

```
KEW  ABLER   PECOS
ORR  BRAGA   EXACT
ARE  HANOI   RESTS
LOSTONESSHIRT
ALTAR      EAST
  BREAKSTHETIE
SPA   ERIN    DUCK
LOX  DELIGHT   BEE
OPEC    FARE    ADS
  BELOWTHEBELT
     THAI   ERASE
  WEARSTHEPANTS
WHIRL  SEENO    GAS
EERIE  ERROR    EVE
TREES  DIDST    REX
```

60

```
THEIR  MAMA   SANK
HORNE  AVIS   ERIE
EPICS  LENIENTLY
  SCHOOLRINGS
    USES   GENTS
SCORNS   ASS    EAT
ARMED  EERO   RAMA
PEALSOFLAUGHTER
PONY  DOLL   REESE
ELI   EER   HEARTS
RESET     AMEN
   BRIDGETOLLS
BARBECUES    BEACH
EPEE  EDNA   LANAI
LOAD  SETS   EDAMS
```

61

```
ACES  BARRE   ABLY
SAME  EPEES   GATE
KNOCKABOUT   ENDS
SATOUT    SPRING
LENDL    ASTUTE
   DOE  PANE   PHI
LOPES  BINGE    JED
IZOD  MOXIE   COME
LOU  LATIN   SOBER
ANN   ASHE    ALE
CEDRIC    BOXES
  CORALS  STILTS
FLAP  RAPSESSION
BIKE  ADORN   TORI
IDES  SETAT   STEP
```

62

```
ALEC  AMOR     PLED
GALL  SADAT   ROSA
EMMA  PHONEBOOTH
SPORTIER   ROMMEL
     KERR   VMI
ROCKNE  HEIL   PGA
EGRET  MART   NILS
ALAN  ROUSE   EVAN
DENT  ELLE   SWORE
SSE  ODDS   LESTER
     STY  SOAP
URSULA  SPORADIC
METROPOLIS   PUMA
PLUG  ELATE   EDAM
SYNE  EVEN   RENE
```

63

```
LPS  SHES   CAGNEY
ALI  CAVE   OPENED
MAN  ALEX   MISERS
PICABOSTREET
STEP   EAT   ACTA
  PAINTTHETOWN
SMATTERS   TEPID
PAT  ORA  AAH  ENE
ALBAN   ECLIPSES
STATEOFGRACE
MAYA  PUG    ROSS
  COUNTRYMUSIC
ADULTS  OHIO   IDO
SEMITE  SEPT   ELO
HIPPOS  SASE   REP
```

64

```
PARS  CASE   TUBAS
ALEC  ODES   ALERT
NASA  RARA   IMAGE
SITTINGBULL   RUE
    SEE   LOBBED
LATVIA   SOARER
ARIAS  FILM   GYPS
NAGS  HELGA   GALE
ABES  ELLA   PANEL
  RARITY  MORTAL
BAWLED    CEL
LEO  MICHAELJFOX
EROSE  HONK   AUDI
AIDED  ABEL   BEEN
TESTY  NOSY   SLAG
```

65

```
ASPS  ADOBE   TWIT
CHAP  LEARN   OHNO
HAILCAESAR   POOR
ERNIE  RICO   ISNT
DITTOS   SELECT
    USED   ASHES
FLAP  VISTAS   ELK
LIL  MEEKEST   RBI
EEL  INSYNC   HEAD
ADAMS    TONE
  BECAME  TULIPS
PLOD  DINT   DINAH
HEAL  EXTRAEXTRA
INRE  PERIL   ERIK
LADY  TRYST   SOSO
```

66

```
BLEND  CBER   EPIC
AUDIO  ARNO   CANE
SKETCHPADS   HIRE
SENATORS   ATONES
    ORA   GREET
CAMERA  WAINSCOT
ODORS  FAZED   HOE
BILE  SIXES   LIZA
RED  DELED   COPES
AUSPICES   MOUSSE
  PEROT   TAU
WOODEN  SOCRATES
OKRA  DRAWSTRAWS
RIEN  LUGE   ELMER
NEST  YEAR   DOERS
```

67

```
SOFAR  PAIL   FAST
ABIDE  ERMA   ALPO
WIDOWSPEAK   LIAR
NEO  ICEAGE   CENT
   SRO   SERMONS
SEQUELS    SIN
OVUM  DOCS   ACHED
REAM  SOULS   RARE
TRYIT  NEAT   ERIN
   TAP   PASSKEY
HOTTISH    NET
LANA  SNOOZE   SBA
EVIL  TOPBANANAS
NECK  OREO   TRICK
ONES  LESE   OATHS
```

68

```
PASTA  THEM   ROTC
ARIES  HALO   EZRA
WELLHEELED   TOAD
NAT   STAGE   ONCE
  ONEASYSTREET
ASTRAL     TOT
REHAB  MAJOR   HOT
IRANI  OWE   OBESE
DAN  STEED   NURSE
   ACE   STREAM
  HIGHONTHEHOG
ACRE  NEATO   LOU
BOER  INTHECHIPS
ISAN  STEN   DONEE
TATE  TODO   SPEND
```

69

S	A	R	I		L	O	A	M	Y		S	K	A	T
E	L	A	N		I	N	N	E	R		E	E	R	O
T	O	M	S		S	T	E	W	S		A	T	T	Y
S	U	P	E	R	B	O	W	L		E	S	T	E	S
			R	O	O			A	R	I	L			
N	E	P	T	U	N	E		S	U	E	D	E	S	
A	V	A	S	T		N	E	A	T		E	D	A	M
P	I	N		I	D	A	H	O		R	U	E		
E	C	H	O		T	E	R	I		S	T	U	N	S
	T	A	B	L	E	D		B	A	H	A	M	A	S
			N	E	E	R			L	O	X			
A	D	D	L	E		P	O	T	B	O	I	L	E	R
M	A	L	I		S	E	P	I	A		C	O	V	E
A	D	E	S		A	L	I	E	N		A	B	E	D
H	A	R	K		L	E	E	R	Y		B	O	S	S

70

T	A	X	I	S		T	V	S		A	D	D	E	R
A	R	E	N	A		H	I	M		P	I	A	N	O
D	I	S	K	D	R	I	V	E		O	N	I	O	N
				D	O	N	A	L	D		L	C	D	
G	A	D	G	E	T	S		T	A	L	L	Y	H	O
U	N	I	O	N	S				R	A	I	D		
I	N	N	O			W	A	T	E	R	P	O	L	O
D	E	N		D	R	I	P	D	R	Y		U	A	R
E	X	E	C	R	A	T	E	S			A	B	B	A
			R	E	E	K			J	O	B	L	O	T
E	N	D	O	W	E	R		S	I	N	C	E	R	E
L	O	A			S	I	M	I	L	E				
F	O	N	D	A		D	U	S	T	D	E	V	I	L
I	N	C	A	N		E	S	S		A	L	I	C	E
N	E	E	D	Y			S	T	Y		Y	I	P	E	S

71

E	L	L	E		T	H	O	M		K	A	F	K	A
V	A	I	L		H	A	L	O		A	R	I	E	L
A	M	M	O		E	R	G	O		S	E	L	E	S
P	E	N	N	Y	M	A	R	S	H	A	L	L		
			G	E	L	S			H	A	S			
S	H	A	W	L		T	R	U			R	P	M	
E	L	I	T	E			P	O	O	L		S	H	E	A
G	E	N	E	R	A	L	Q	U	A	R	T	E	R	S
O	P	E	D		B	O	U	T		O	A	T	E	S
S	T	S		A	W	E			B	U	N	T	S	
			A	S	S			S	A	N	D			
N	I	C	K	E	L	A	N	D	D	I	M	E		
M	A	N	T	A		A	D	A	M		N	O	S	H
A	S	C	O	T		M	I	K	E		G	A	T	E
S	H	A	R	E		A	M	E	N		S	T	A	Y

72

F	I	R	S	T		A	L	S		M	A	S	K	S
A	L	O	H	A		Y	E	A		A	V	A	I	L
T	A	M	E	R		L	A	W		R	O	D	E	O
	P	E	R	M	A	N	E	N	T	W	A	V	E	
			P	I	E			D	E	I				
U	S	O		E	M	I	R		E	N	A	M	E	L
T	I	D	E	S	O	V	E	R		I	T	A	L	O
I	G	O	R			E	G	O			O	N	E	S
C	H	R	I	S			S	A	L	T	A	M	I	N	E
A	S	S	E	N	T			L	E	A	P		C	A	R
			E	O	S				P	T	S			
C	U	R	R	E	N	T	E	V	E	N	T	S		
O	S	I	E	R		O	W	E		E	A	T	E	R
L	E	O	N	E		R	E	T		S	K	A	T	E
A	S	T	O	R		Y	R	S		S	E	R	A	C

73

L	O	C	H		A	C	T	O	R		Z	A	N	E
A	G	R	A		L	O	R	N	E		A	D	A	Y
D	E	E	P		E	N	A	C	T		M	O	R	E
Y	E	A		C	R	E	P	E	R	U	B	B	E	R
			M	E	E	T	S			E	R	I	E	S
A	S	P	E	N	S			D	I	A	N	A		
F	A	U	L	T		W	E	L	D	S		E	A	T
A	R	F	S		H	I	L	L	S		Y	A	R	E
R	A	F		R	O	L	L	S		L	A	S	E	R
			R	E	E	D	S		B	U	N	Y	A	N
S	P	E	N	D				P	A	R	K	A		
P	I	E	C	E	O	F	C	A	K	E		S	P	A
E	R	N	E		W	A	I	V	E		S	P	I	N
S	E	C	S		N	I	T	E	R		K	I	C	K
O	N	E	S		S	L	E	D	S		Y	E	A	H

74

A	T	R	I	P		F	E	R	A	L		U	P	S
C	H	I	M	E		O	N	I	C	E		S	U	M
T	R	A	P	P	E	R	J	O	H	N		E	R	E
S	U	L	U		T	A	O			A	R	E	A	
			D	O	O	G	I	E	H	O	W	S	E	R
A	M	E	R			E	N	C	O	R	E			
S	C	E	N	I	C			S	O	L	D		S	G	T
P	I	S	T	O	L	S				N	E	E	D	L	E	R
A	D	S		L	E	I	S		D	R	E	A	M	Y
			P	E	R	S	I	A			E	F	T	S
J	A	M	E	S	K	I	L	D	A	R	E			
O	D	O	R			I	D	S		R	O	A	D	
L	O	X		M	A	R	C	U	S	W	E	L	B	Y
T	R	I		A	D	H	O	C		A	N	D	I	E
S	E	E		O	Z	O	N	E		S	T	E	E	R

75

E	B	B	S		A	L	L	I			C	R	O	
L	O	O	K		N	O	O	N	E		I	R	A	S
B	O	X	I	N	G	R	I	N	G		N	O	S	H
A	N	Y		O	L	D	S		G	O	T	C	H	A
	B	U	O	Y				A	R	C	H			
M	A	S	O	N	S		P	R	O	T	E	S	T	S
A	L	T	O	S		M	A	I	L			C	L	I	P
S	L	A	M		G	A	V	E	L		L	A	N	E
T	A	R	O		O	N	E	S		S	I	N	G	E
S	H	E	R	W	O	O	D		H	I	N	T	E	D
			B	I	F	F		P	O	R	K			
S	U	N	U	N	U		S	A	M	E		F	L	U
O	T	I	S		P	O	P	S	I	N	G	L	E	S
W	A	N	T		S	A	U	T	E		N	O	N	E
S	H	E			T	R	E	S			P	E	A	R

76

O	S	C	A	R		M	E	C	C	A		D	O	S
A	P	A	C	E		A	S	H	E	S		O	W	L
H	U	S	H	P	U	P	P	I	E	S		G	N	U
U	N	S	E	E	M	L	Y			U	P	P	E	R
				A	P	E		M	O	R	T	A	R	
F	A	C	E	T	S			R	E	R	E	A	D	
U	R	A	L	S		C	O	A	L	S		D	N	A
N	E	T	S		T	H	A	N	E		B	L	O	T
D	A	B		C	R	E	S	T		B	U	E	N	O
	U	P	L	I	F	T		S	O	D	D	E	N	
T	R	O	O	P	S			S	P	Y				
L	O	G	I	C		E	L	E	C	T	I	N	G	
A	W	L		K	I	T	T	Y	C	O	R	N	E	R
T	E	A		E	L	A	T	E		T	E	N	S	E
E	R	R		R	A	D	A	R		T	E	S	T	Y

77

A	L	A	N		D	I	P	S		P	A	C	E	S
L	I	L	A		E	R	I	E		A	B	O	D	E
T	E	L	E	S	C	O	P	E		G	A	U	N	T
A	G	E		C	A	N	E	D		E	T	N	A	S
R	E	N	T	E	D			S	A	B	O	T		
			A	N	E	A	R		C	O	R	D	E	D
U	N	C	L	E		T	A	S	T	Y		O	P	A
P	E	A	L		H	O	C	K	S		O	W	E	D
D	A	N		C	O	N	E	Y		R	U	N	E	S
	O	R	A	C	L	E		R	E	B	E	C		
			V	O	I	D	S		O	T	H	E	R	S
S	T	E	V	E		I	A	M	B	I		L	E	A
L	O	R	E	N		S	P	A	C	E	S	U	I	T
A	P	A	R	T		A	S	I	A		E	D	G	E
M	E	L	T	S			L	E	N	T		W	E	N	D

78

C	A	N	A	R	Y		B	I	T	E		P	L	O
E	L	A	I	N	E		A	C	E	D		L	E	A
L	E	M	M	A	S		K	I	D	S	T	U	F	F
T	R	E	S			D	E	E	D		E	M	T	S
S	T	R	A	W	B	E	R	R	Y	J	A	M		
				T	H	E	M			U	S	E	R	
A	F	B		E	N	O	C	H		J	E	T	E	R
T	O	E	A	R			T	O	A		I	D	E	A	L
T	R	A	D	E		E	G	R	E	T		D	D	S
	K	N	O	T			A	S	S	T				
		P	R	O	F	I	T	S	Q	U	E	E	Z	E
S	H	O	E		E	N	O	S		S	L	O	W	
C	O	L	D	P	A	C	K		I	N	T	U	N	E
A	N	E		I	S	A	Y		F	E	E	D	E	R
B	K	S		A	T	N	O			S	T	R	E	S	S

79

S	L	I	P		P	E	E	L	S		F	A	C	T
W	A	V	E		A	R	R	O	W		I	L	A	Y
A	V	A	N	T	G	A	R	D	E		L	I	S	P
P	I	N		W	A	S		G	A	Z	E	T	T	E
			S	E	A	S	O	N		P	E	R	O	T
	A	S	I	D	E			S	O	M	B	E	R	
S	L	A	V		N	O	R	M		M	I	A	M	I
H	O	B	O		I	N	S	E	T		G	R	U	B
O	N	E	I	F		T	O	G	A		N	E	S	S
P	E	T	R	O	L			N	A	R	C	O		
			F	R	E	E	S		H	O	N	C	H	O
A	V	I	A	T	O	R		N	E	U		R	U	B
Z	I	T	I		N	O	M	D	E	P	L	U	M	E
U	S	E	R		I	D	E	A	L		I	D	O	S
L	A	M	E		D	E	S	K	S		P	E	R	E

80

P	A	S	S		S	C	A	N		P	A	S	T	A
A	R	E	A		K	E	N	O		A	U	T	O	S
R	O	D	T	A	Y	L	O	R		T	R	O	M	P
I	M	A		A	L	E			P	R	I	C	E	S
S	A	N	D	R	A	B	U	L	L	O	C	K		
			R	O	B		M	A	U	L		P	E	Z
T	A	L	O	N		S	P	I	T	S		I	D	A
I	S	U	P		M	O	T	T	O		F	L	I	P
N	I	X		H	A	L	E	Y		D	I	E	T	S
T	A	U		A	L	T	E		A	I	D			
			R	O	L	L	I	N	G	S	T	O	N	E	S
S	W	I	F	T	S			O	T	S		O	L	E
I	R	A	T	E		H	E	N	R	Y	L	U	C	E
L	A	T	E	R		O	R	E	O		A	S	I	N
O	P	E	N	S		P	A	R	S		M	E	D	O

81

```
WEBS·RAND·PARTY
ANEW·EVER·AMUSE
TOGA·CORA·YANKS
CLUBSANDWICH···
HANSEL·NRA·BUT·
···CLOP·ESTATE
SCOOT·TEESHIRTS
COCO·TAX·MEET··
INTHEHOLE·REDRY
ODESSA·ECRU····
NOT·CIA·ASTROS·
···CARRYTHEBALL
CHEAP·MEIR·ANDI
SUSIE·ETNA·REIN
TREND·DISH·SEEK
```

82

```
LOBE·REDS·MIFF
APEX·INRE·EVERT
MATE·FLAN·SOLID
BLACKLIST·ARLES
··NEST·ABYSS··
·SAGE·TIDBIT··
POURED·COO·OPED
EURASIA·OUTWARD
PLAY·ARC·THEIRS
··MCLEAN·URNS·
··FOALS·LOOM··
BRUTE·JOHNBROWN
BUTTE·URIS·CLAY
BITES·MITE·MERE
TORE·PEST·POST
```

83

```
TANG·HARSH·ARAB
ALOE·ALICE·VERA
PAPERTIGER·IDLY
AMAZE·TINE·AMOS
SORELY·DESIRE·
··RYAN···CYNIC
FATS·HORACE·ASH
IRA·COVERED·CLU
SEX·LOAFED·DEEM
HADTO···SAFE··
·ORDERS·REMOTE
ALDA·DANA·DOPES
SIGN·GIANTSTEPS
AVEC·ASIDE·ERIE
PERE·RELAX·DADS
```

84

```
HASP·RAPID·STEM
IDEA·AMORE·TONE
PERRYMASON·AUNT
SNAFU·ZEN·ARGUE
·ACTE··ORCHID·
ATTICUSFINCH··
TARTAN·AVES·DBA
IMUS·DALES·FRAN
TEE·TRES·TOLEDO
··GRACEVANOWEN
·OCHRES··ERST·
WREAK·FIR·EIDER
LAND·BENMATLOCK
ENNE·ASKIN·LOCO
TEAS·STYNE·AMES
```

85

```
EMIT·CRABBE·CEL
GARR·HELLOS·ACE
GRAINOFSALT·NAN
··VIP···STEWARD
EBSEN·CAT·ARTE
CANTATAS·SOLDER
USA··INSTEAD··
·SPLINTERGROUP
·ASTORIA··RAE
GRAPHS·TELECAST
EELS·ASS·MALTA
ATTESTS··HIT··
RIM·WINDSORKNOT
ENA·ARENAS·IRAE
DAN·BERATE·NATE
```

86

```
WIFE·GRIST·FIST
HOES·RECUR·ASTA
AUNTIEMAME·TEAM
MSS·REIN·SPHERE
··SENT··SPEE··
STAINS··CHAIRMAN
LAPSE·DUES·GONE
ALOT·HERES·ODDS
TORE·OUST·COURT
ENTRANCE·LASSES
··KNEE··RICE··
SAFETY·MACH·OSU
ATAN·BROTHERRAT
BORN·EERIE·YALE
EMMY·ELTON·ELKS
```

87

```
BABY·THOR·BOGIE
AWEE·RENO·EARLS
RHEA·AREA·ATILT
KITTYCORNERED·
ALLSET··VENICE
TEE·MIA·EAR·ROD
··LEONID··OOPS
SPINNINGJENNY·
JOAD··STEAMS··
OAR·ERE·RPI·KOS
GREENE··ALPINE
·NERVOUSNELLIE
INTRO·KNEE·ATOM
TRAIL·ADES·TENT
TALES·YORE·ORSO
```

88

```
TEDS·RASP·MADAM
IDEA·ELLA·ALICE
BELL·JOANRIVERS
INTL·OHM·ELATES
ASSYRIA··ATE··
··FAN·APERTURE
GENIE·CLASSICAL
OBIE·SHIRT·GLUM
BALLPOINT·SEALS
INEDIBLE·CTR··
··EEL·DRAWERS·
SPRIER·FOE·OREO
PAULYSHORE·OREL
ANNIE·DRIP·DOSE
STEAD·LEAS·SLED
```

89

```
ABEL·ACHE·PALS
BOLA·SLEET·ECOL
AGUN·TERRA·DENY
FIDDLEAROUND··
TEE·ERN··ELATE
··HESSE·FEELER
ASTOR·ONME·TRI
BLOWYOUROWNHORN
NAP·ATON·EASES
EVILER·LONGS··
RECON··TAE·ALA
·GETGOODVIBES
SARA·ALONE·LEAN
EVEN·MINER·SAVE
WADS··BASS·AMER
```

90

```
RIPPLE·ONE·UGH
AMORAL·REVENUE
JASONALEXANDER
AGED·TILT·DOS·
HES·PEN·TDS·SPA
··FIDELIO·SWAN
IMAN··EMU··PONY
VICTORHERBERT·
RANT·TEA··ELKS
ENCS·TARHEEL··
MAE·DOC·ALT·CPA
·MIR·TARP·ANON
BENEDICTARNOLD
SARDINE··SETTLE
ATE·MGS·OBSESS
```

91

```
TARP·STRIFE·DDS
ETUI·TAILOR·REP
NONETOOSOON·INA
··RAP·ENDEAVOR
ADORN·BRA·METE
VINEGAR··ALINES
ANT··LOURDES··
·SOMELIKEITHOT
··ABILENE··TRA
CANTBE··TUMMIES
ADAR·ELS·EASES
SEMINOLE··FAD·
BSA·ALLFALLDOWN
ATT·PLATTE·ERIE
HEH·SASSED·RENE
```

92

```
HOPE·GAZER·MASK
OXEN·OPINE·UGLI
MIND·VENOM·PEAL
EDT·JEDCLAMPETT
REAPER··ROE··
·MAANDPAKETTLE
STERN·ROME·SHOW
HAT·CAWED·USE·
ACES·OPEN·HUNTS
MORTIMERSNERD·
··ENE··ERNEST
LUMANDABNER·RAH
ORAL·IREAD·ABBA
OGLE·AGATE·WALT
PEER·NOTED·EYES
```

93

```
GAS   BWANA HASTA
LOT   EATEN ENTER
ORR   CHANNELSURF
STACK      EIRE
SAILORS   ERNEST
  TUNEIN  SALOON
SOL  SORES   KUDO
AMAN SEPAL  SNAP
LACE   NATAL  DYE
THEMES  LURERS
 ADONIS  PAPAYAS
  ALES     ANSEL
COVEMOLDING  TRI
ADORE  LAINE  EIN
NEWEL  SKIES  MEG
```

94

```
INLAW HUMAN  NEW
ABIDE ERASE  OVA
MADEAPASSAT  ROT
    KARAT   PIKE
SNIDEST   ABUSER
PUTONTHEBLOCK
EDAMS    NOVAK
DELI TANYA  ENID
  NEHRU   TRITE
GOTAKICKOUTOF
MCLEAN   REOPENS
ALAS    ICANT
CAN  HADONTHERUN
ARC  ALLEN  ELITE
WEE  WEEDY  DOMED
```

95

```
TALE  SCOOP  ELBE
RUED  HELLO  NERO
ARGO  IDLER  JEAN
MAP  BREASTWORKS
   USERS   RAISE
TALONS    SWAIN
ALLOT  BERYL  WIS
DIET  DOMES  MINT
SER  LENIN  DANCE
  LACES   SOUGHT
  COATI   STOIC
THIGHMASTER  HOT
YALE  AWARE  MAGI
PIER  LOVED  DIEM
ENDS  SLEWS  TREE
```

96

```
PAST  BLOT  SHAVE
OGLE  LIRA  CIGAR
DRUMSUPBUSINESS
SAMPLE  SPA   DDE
   TUMS    ELIS
LBS  ROAR  EVICTS
OOPS  OVER  AGREE
TOOTONESOWNHORN
STRIP  DISH  TORS
ASTRAL  NEIL  NYE
   FLOP   STAR
UAR  NAP   ELISHA
STRINGSATTACHED
AIMEE  TIKI  HIRE
CLYDE  ALOE  ENOS
```

97

```
SHAHS  IDO  CLAWS
HOSEA  RAP  LITRE
APART  ARE  UNTIE
WINDINSTRUMENT
    SRI    ALP
OFF  ICES  METTLE
RAINCHECK   DARED
ERLE  ELENA  CAYS
ACERB  SNOWWHITE
DETOUR TBAR  TEL
    IAN    RES
HAILTOTHECHIEF
WOUND  BOA  KENYA
HEDGE  LIL  EATEN
OSIER  ELL  DROSS
```

98

```
TOPO  GRACE  HUSH
ENOS  LENOX  OHIO
SMOKEANDMIRRORS
HERALD  SPLASHES
    RAIL   SEG
OPS  LOIS  STAFFS
MICA  LSTS  ABOIL
INABLAZEOFGLORY
TURBO  TERI  ELSE
SPEECH DELL  STR
    AEC   SMEE
TOASTERS  GALLOP
INTHELINEOFFIRE
MOTO  EMOTE  IVES
ERAT  DEBAR  NEST
```

99

```
SAGE  ACTUP  CLAW
EGOS  SHIRE  HESA
MOOS  SINGE  IVAN
INN  GUTTERSNIPE
SYSTEMS    LET
  TORE   FREEZING
HAREM  FRISK  WAR
AXIS  SLOPS  DAME
ILK  BEANS  KESEY
LEEGRANT   JEFF
  OAF   PAPYRUS
BANANASPLIT  ASA
OMIT  RURAL  AMIN
RENE  EMOTE  LEND
KNEE  ROWED  EDGY
```

100

```
GIST   DRAW  GABS
INCA  DIANA  ESAU
SNAPDRAGON  TERI
MEL  OISE  DECANT
ORACLE   SMEAR
    REDS  ARRANGE
SALAD  POPE  COOT
ELIS  WOULD  KONA
LASH  ARTE  SINES
LITHEST   SPIN
  ETHYL  EDGING
AZALEA  OGRE  OAR
GERM  BREAKDANCE
ERNE  LISPS  LIRE
SOOT  EASE   ICED
```